The Diary Of A Photographer

Volume 1: Water Lilies

By

Charles Pfoutz

All Pictures Captured By
Charles Pfoutz

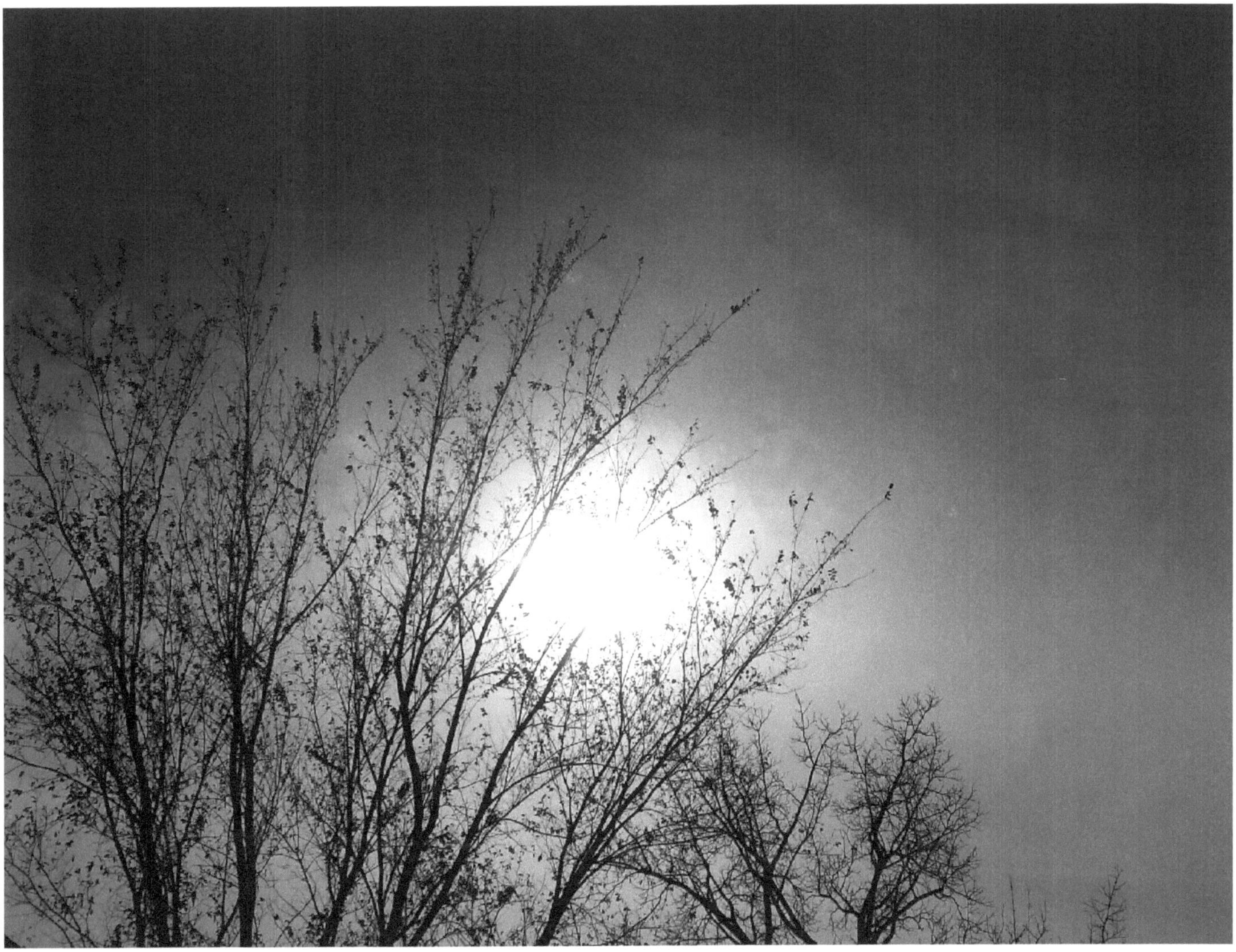

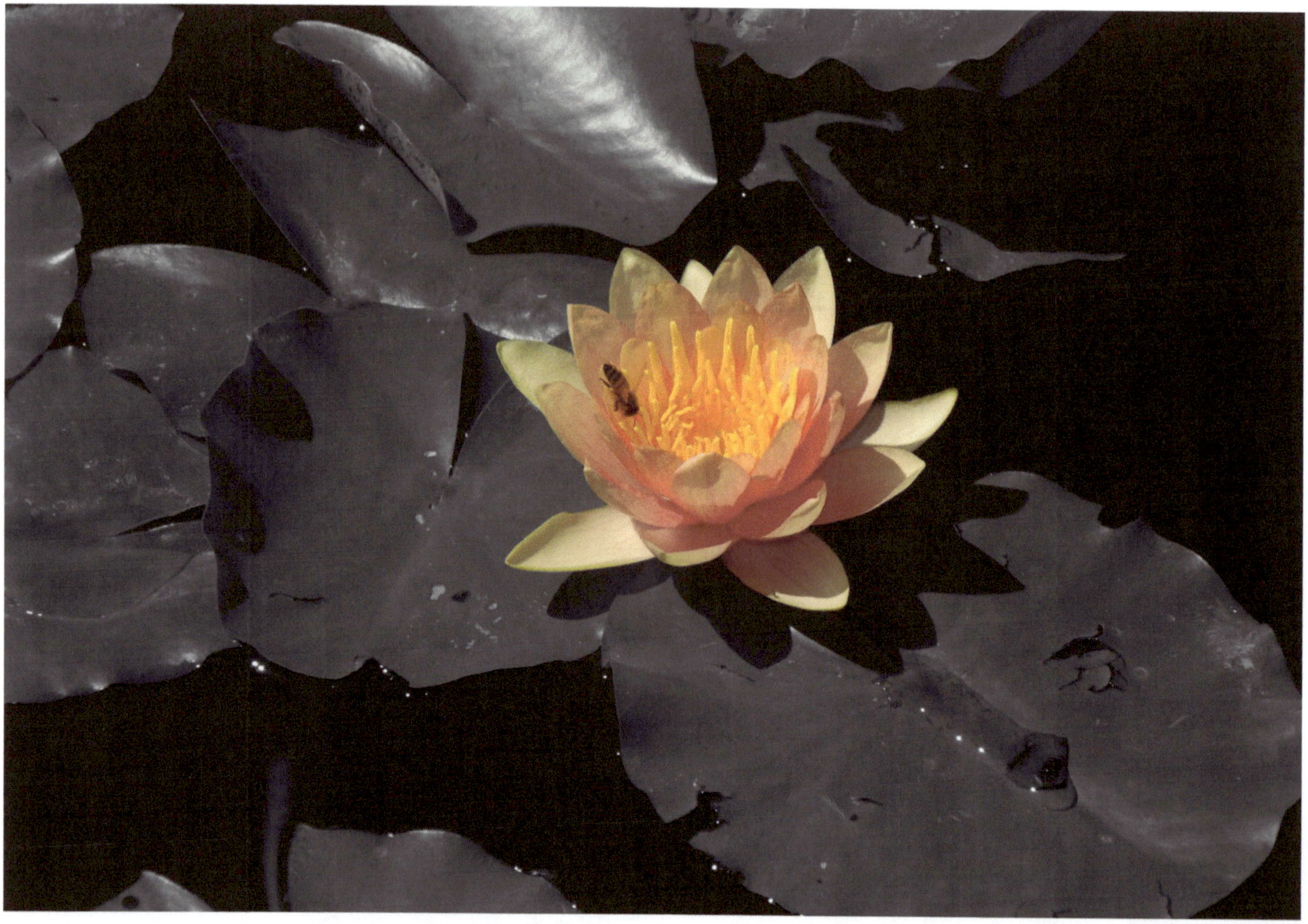

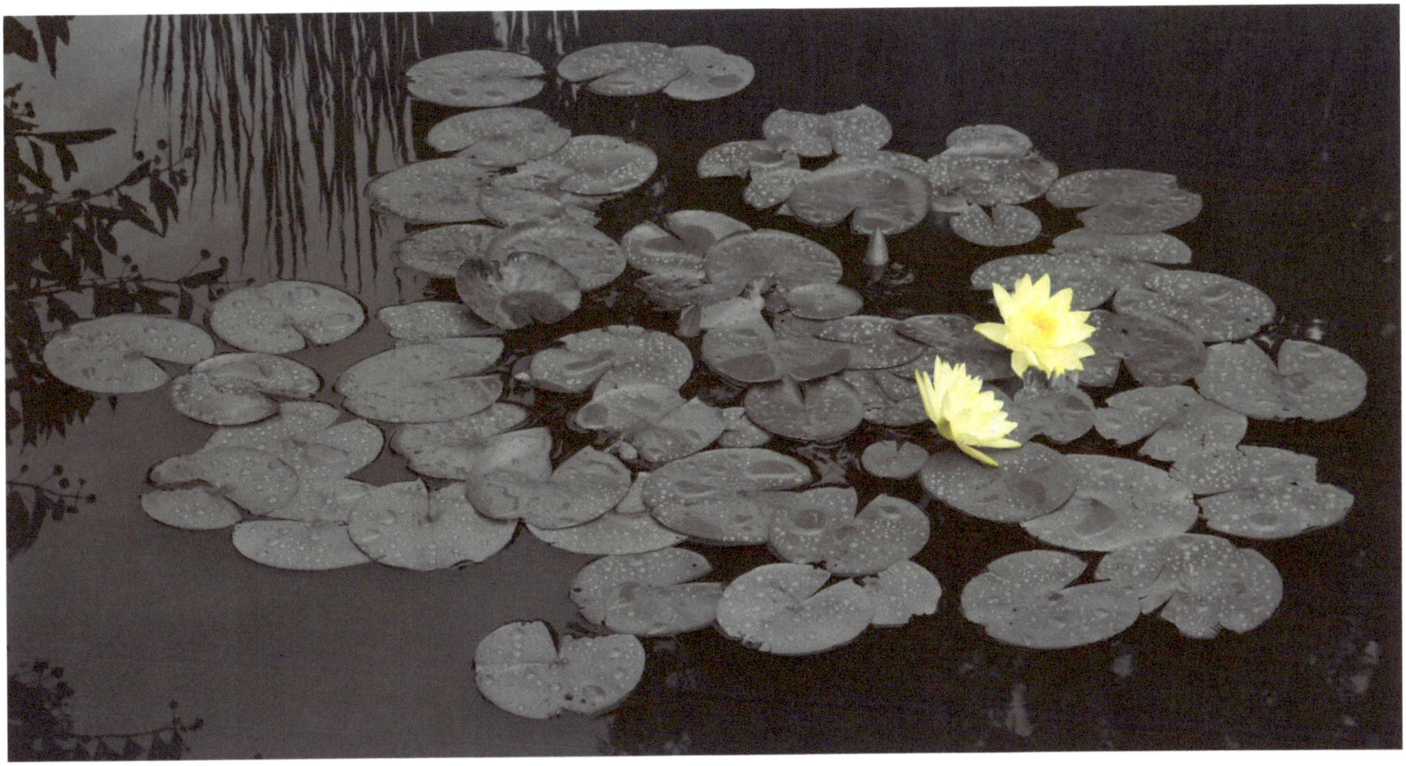

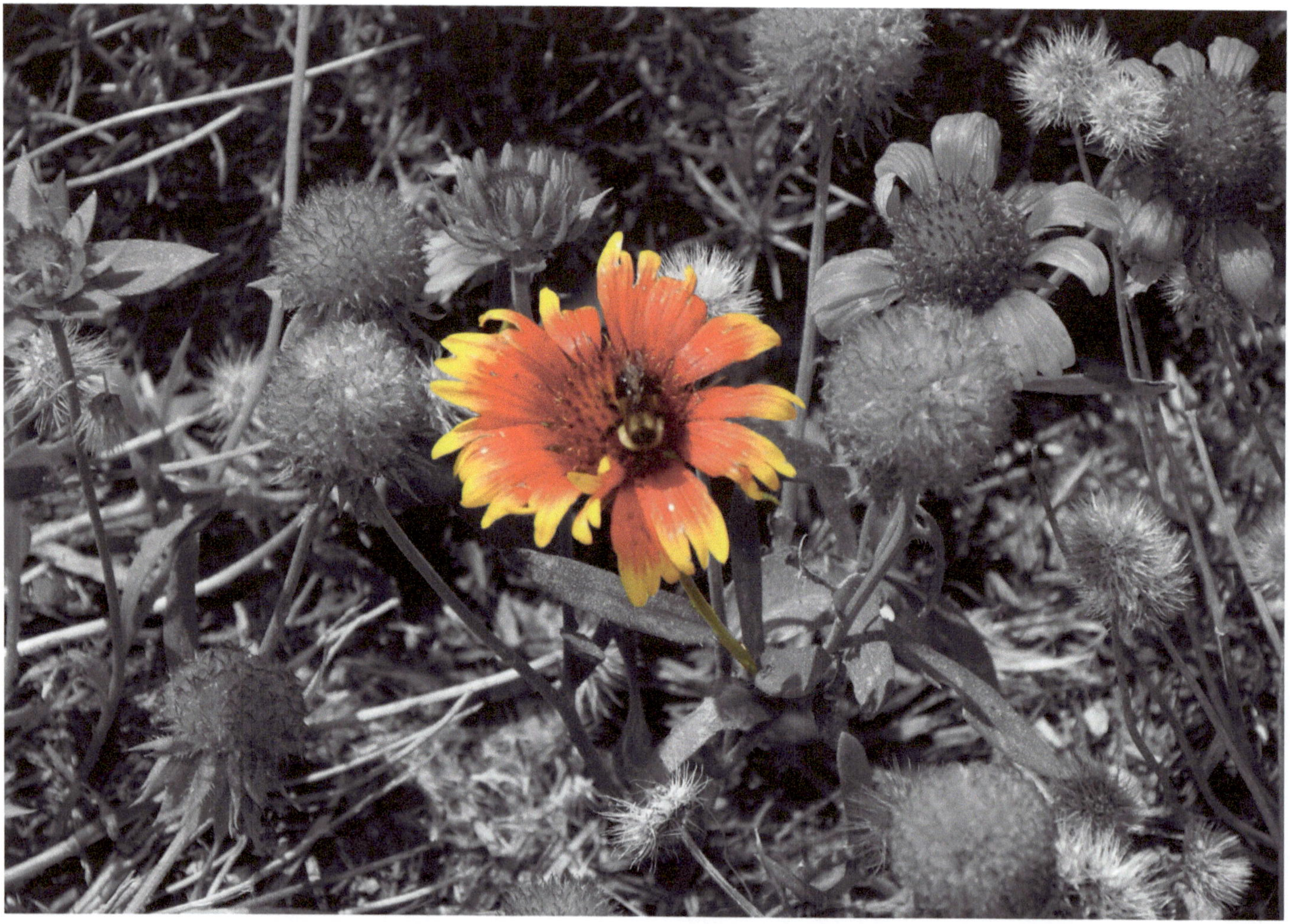

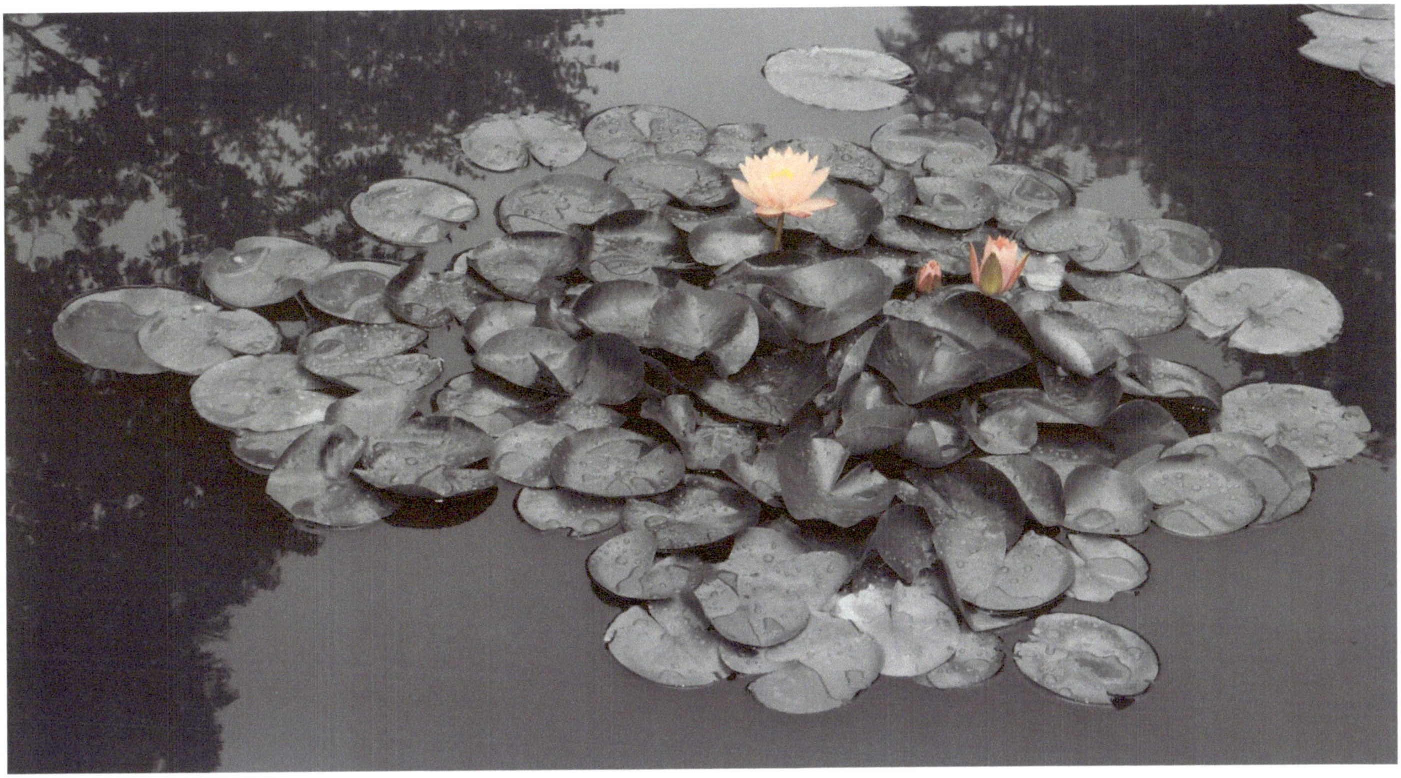

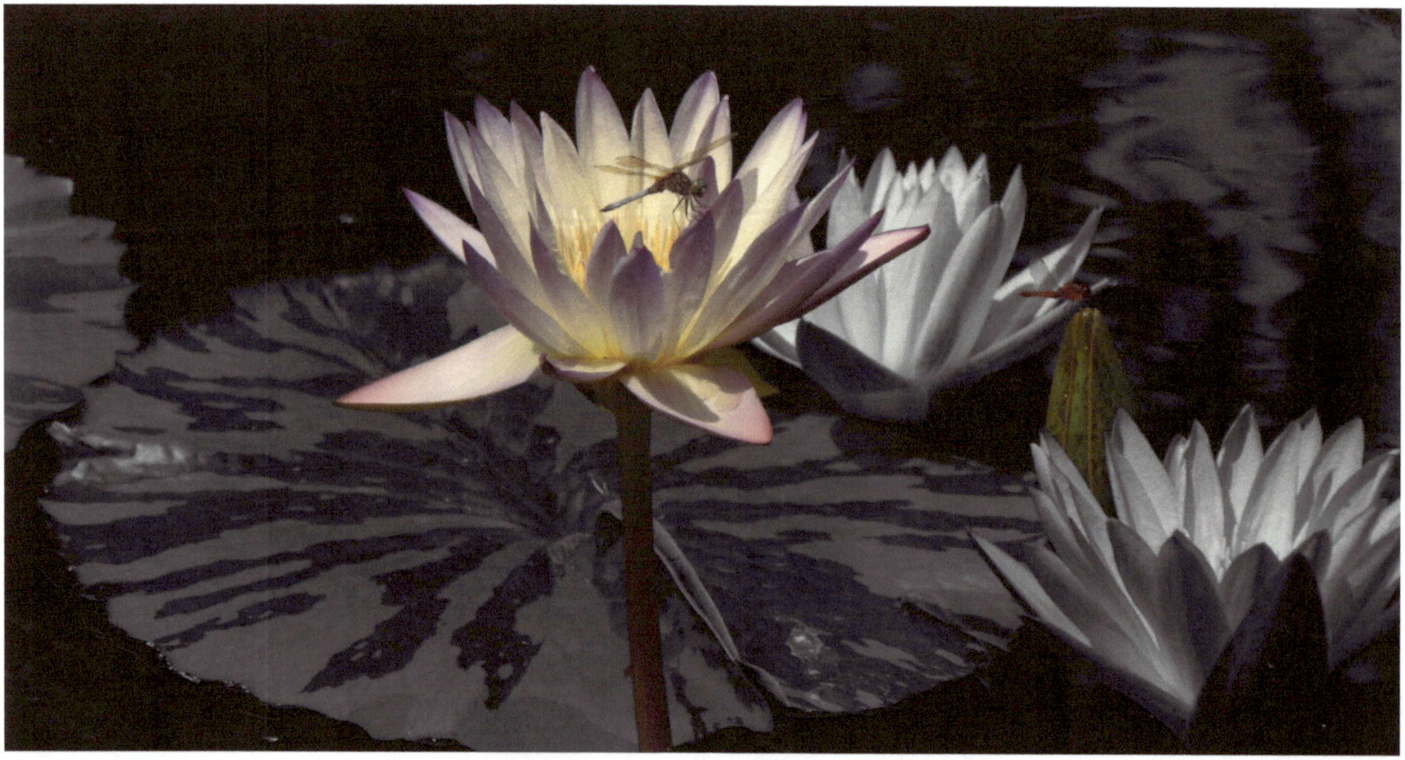

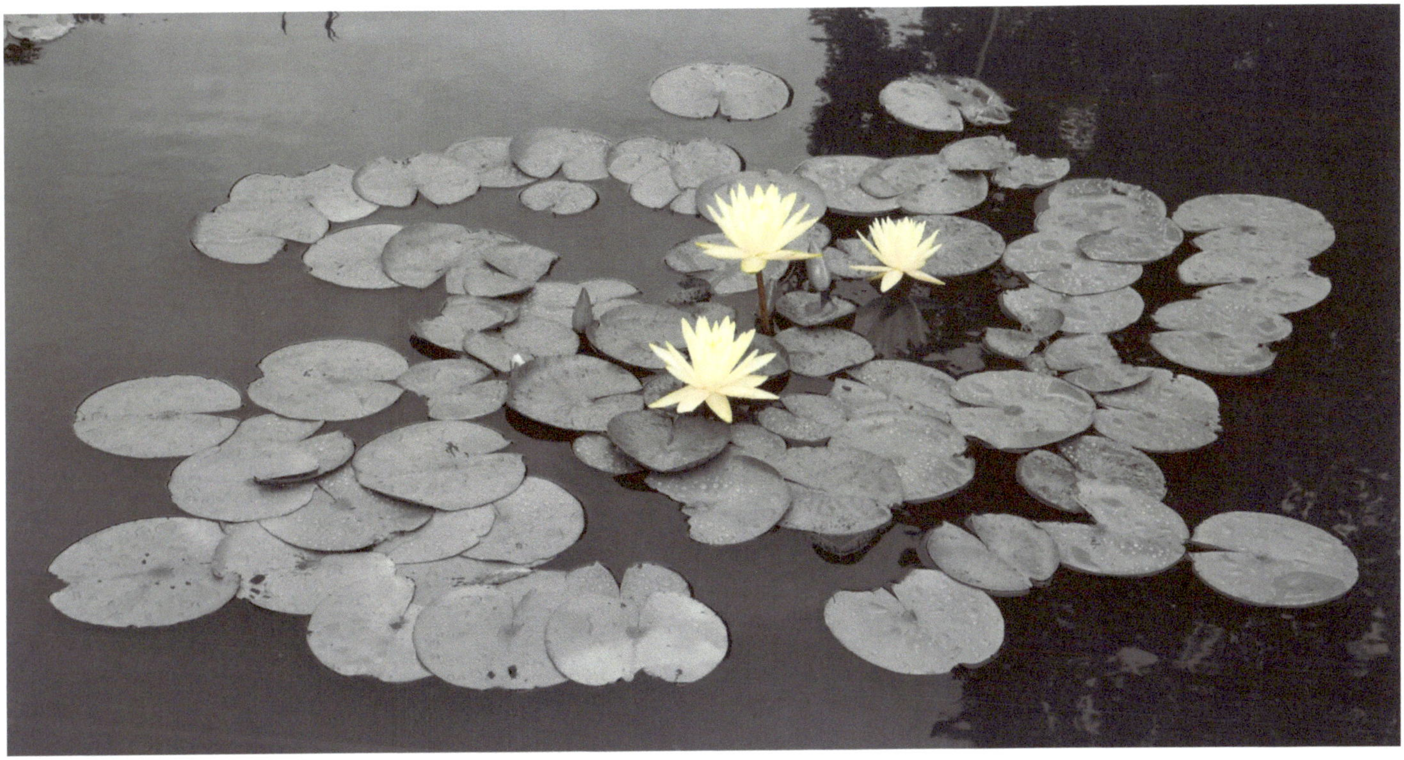

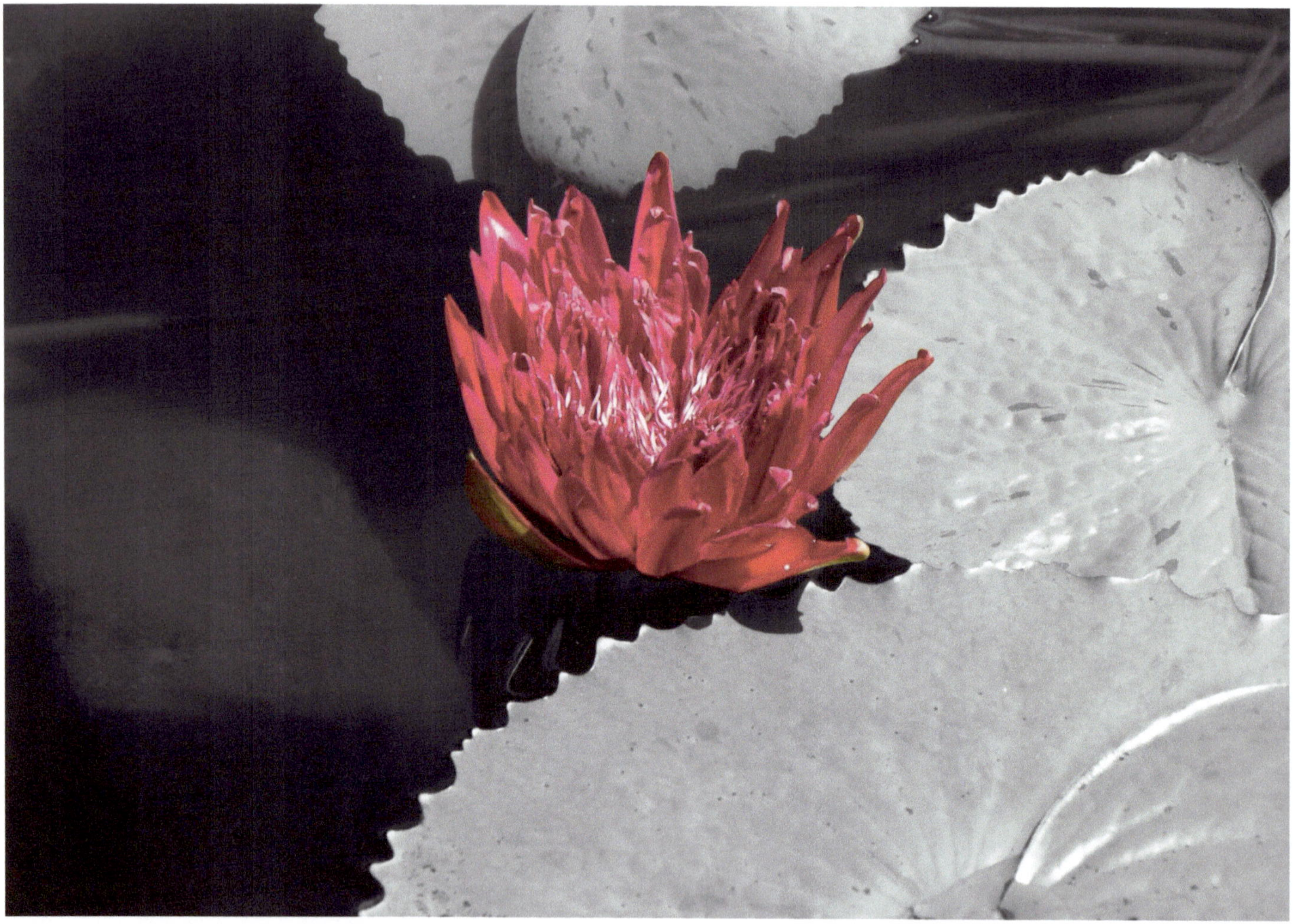

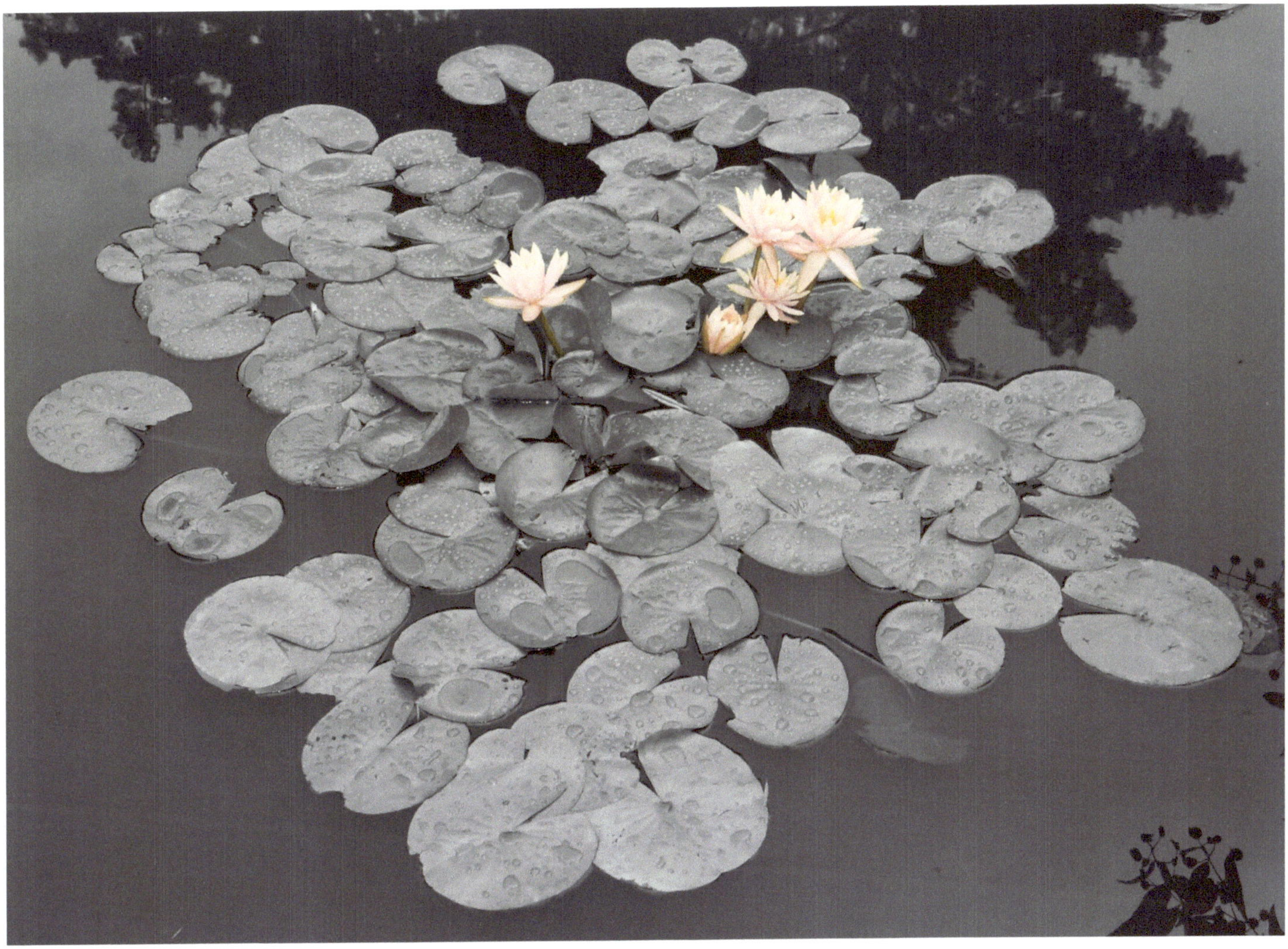

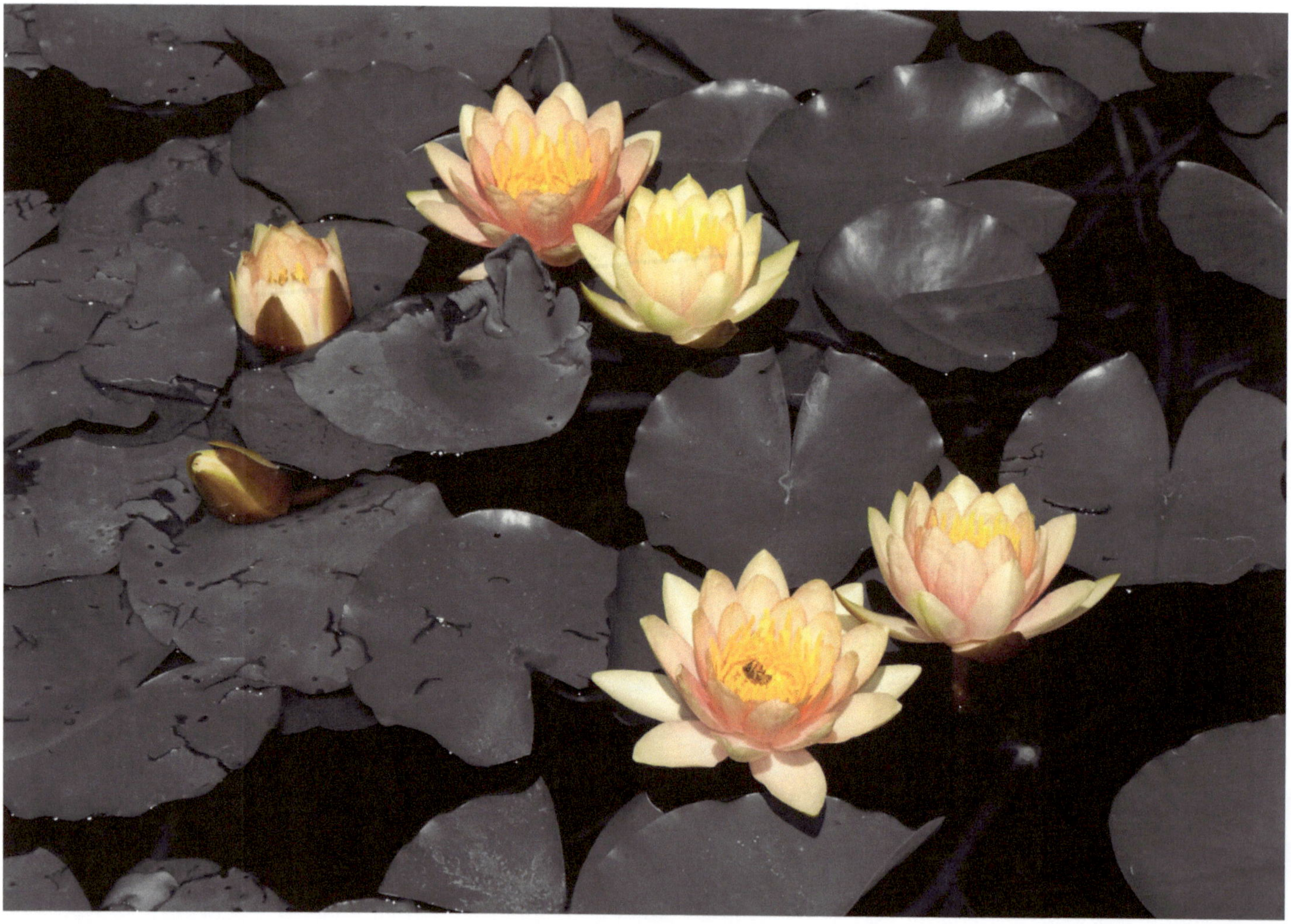

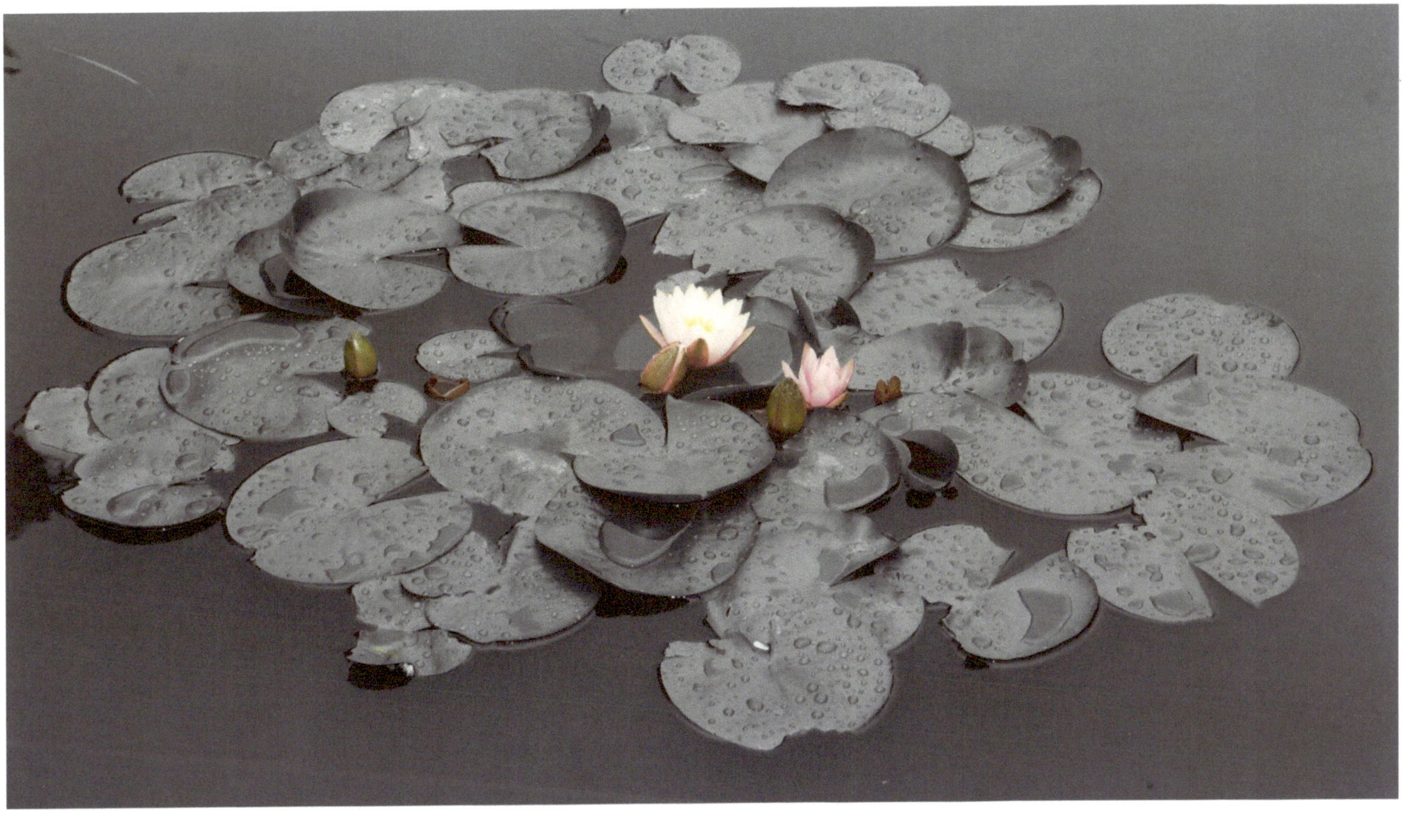

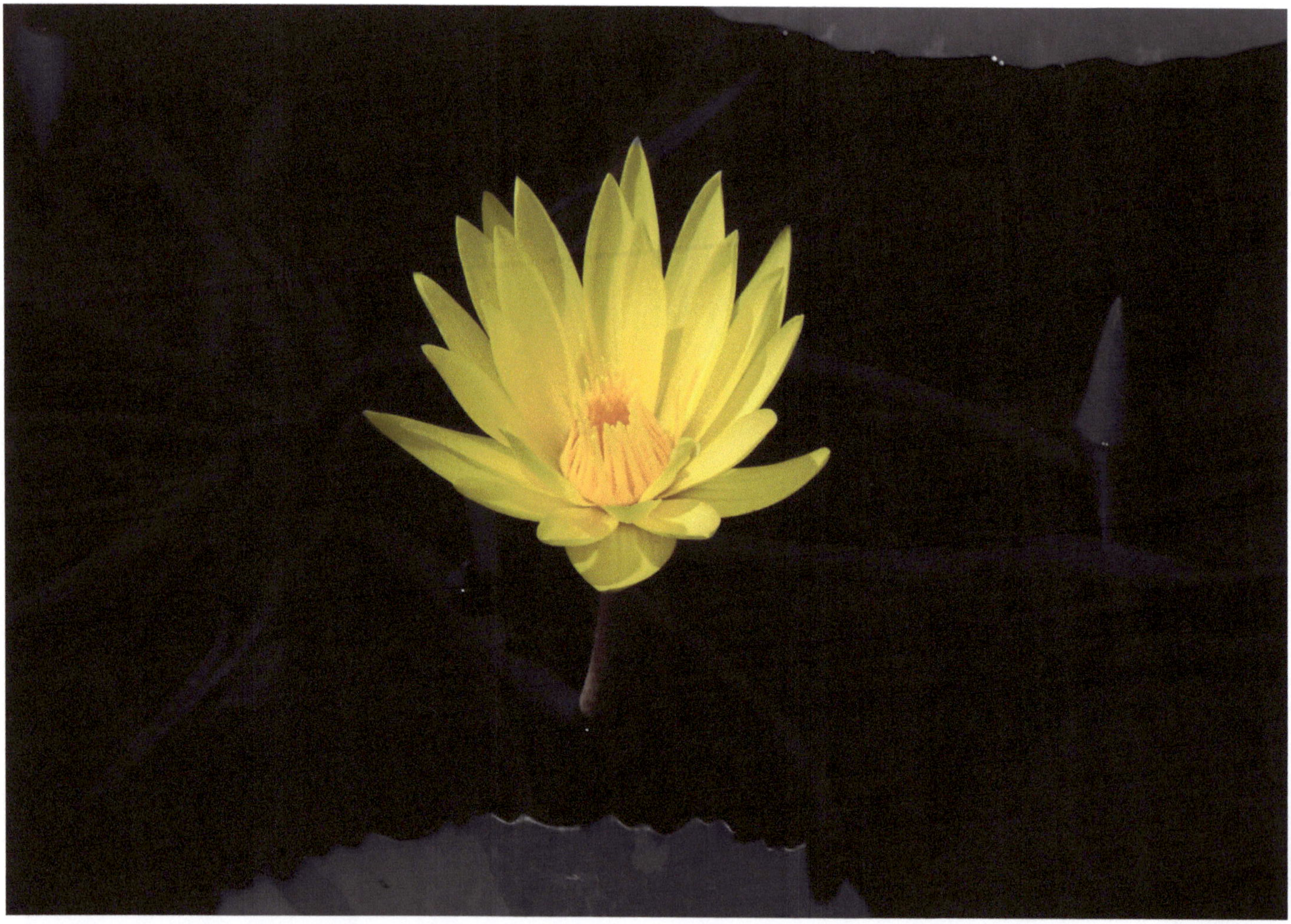

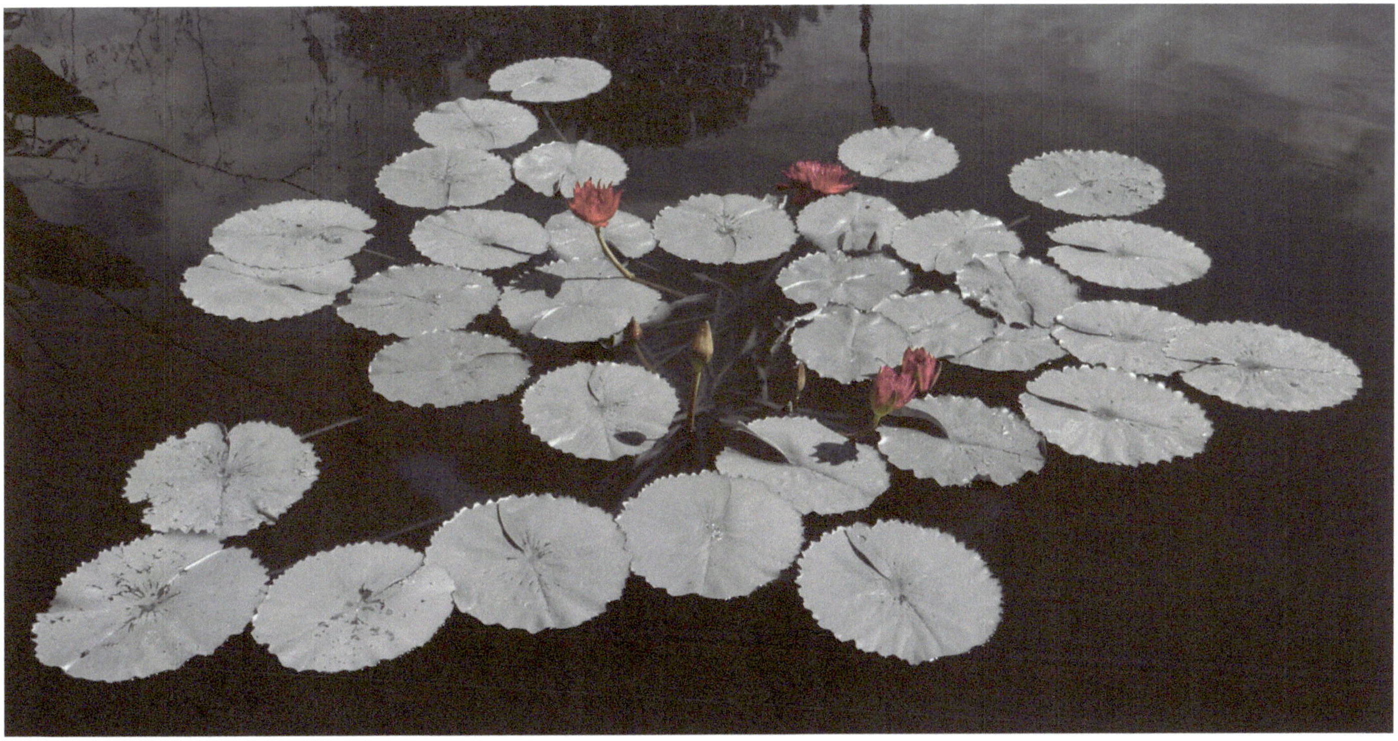

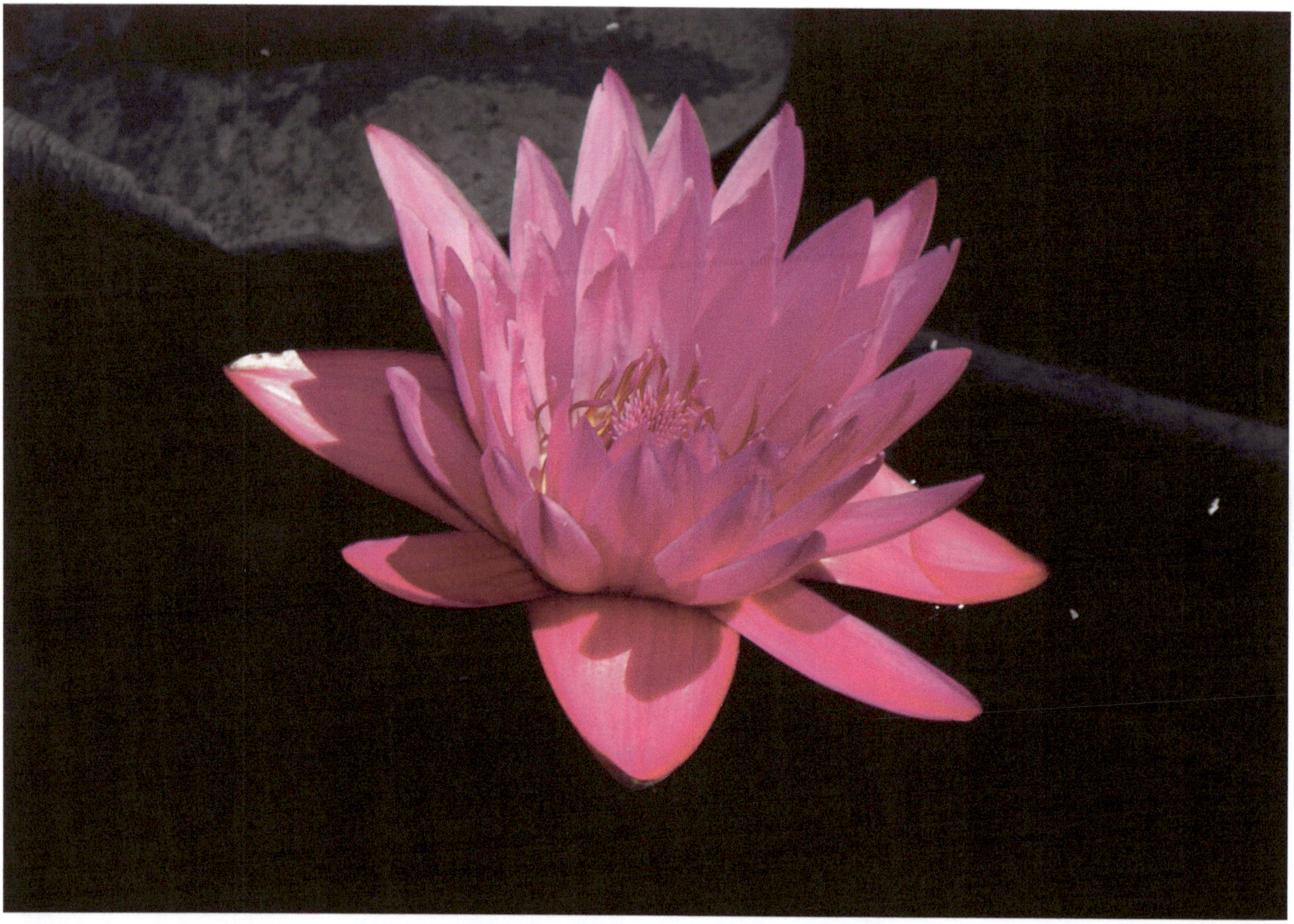

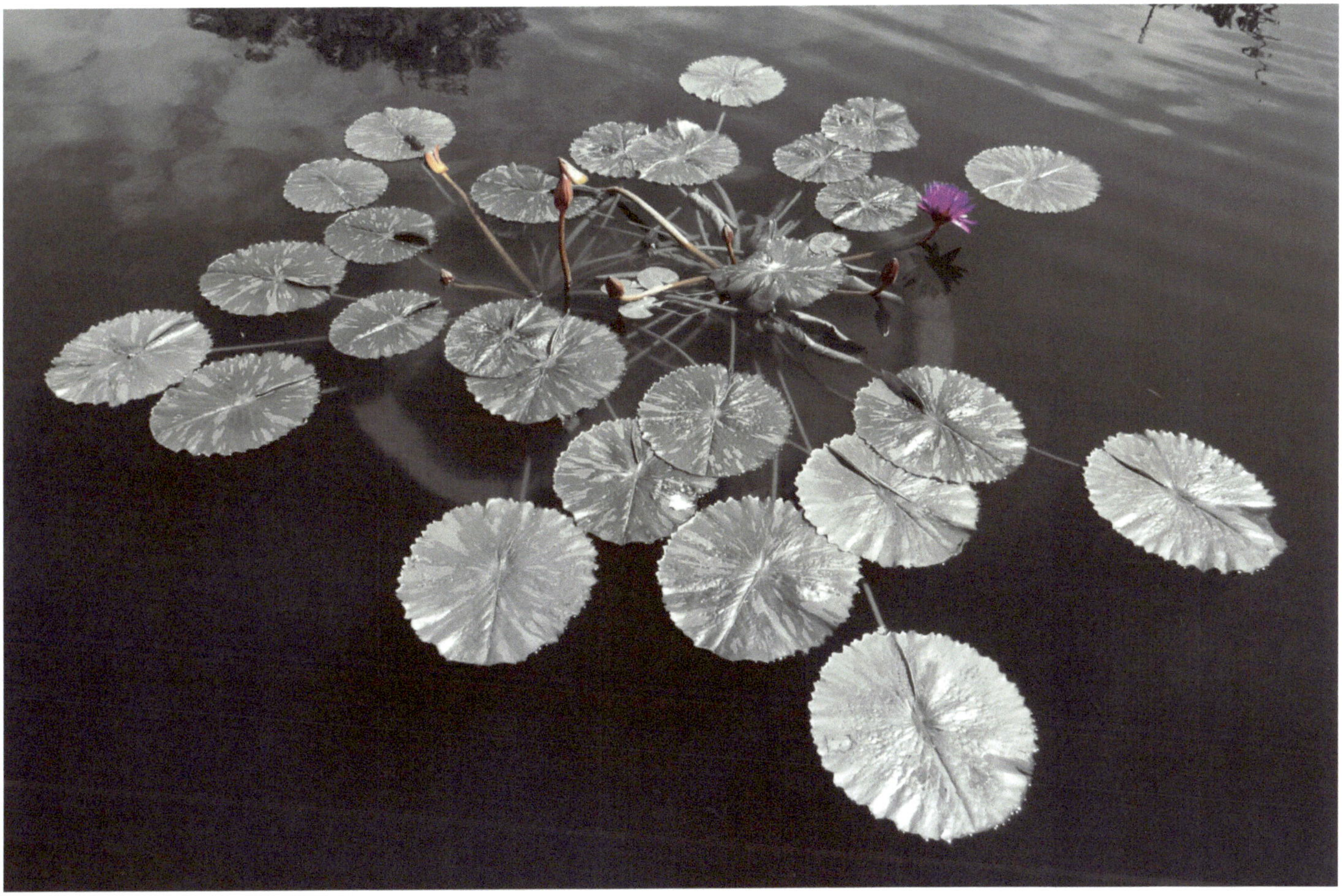

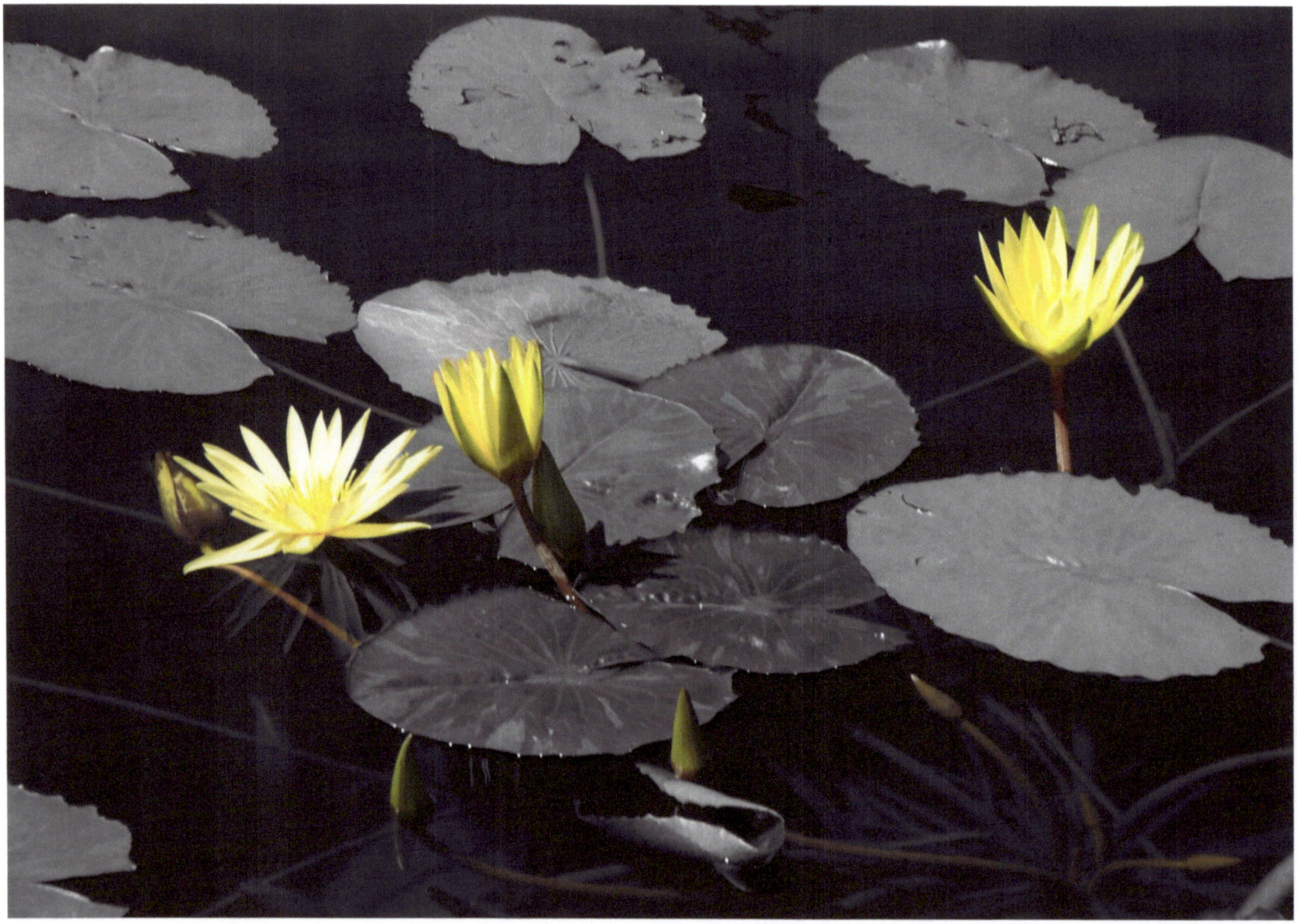

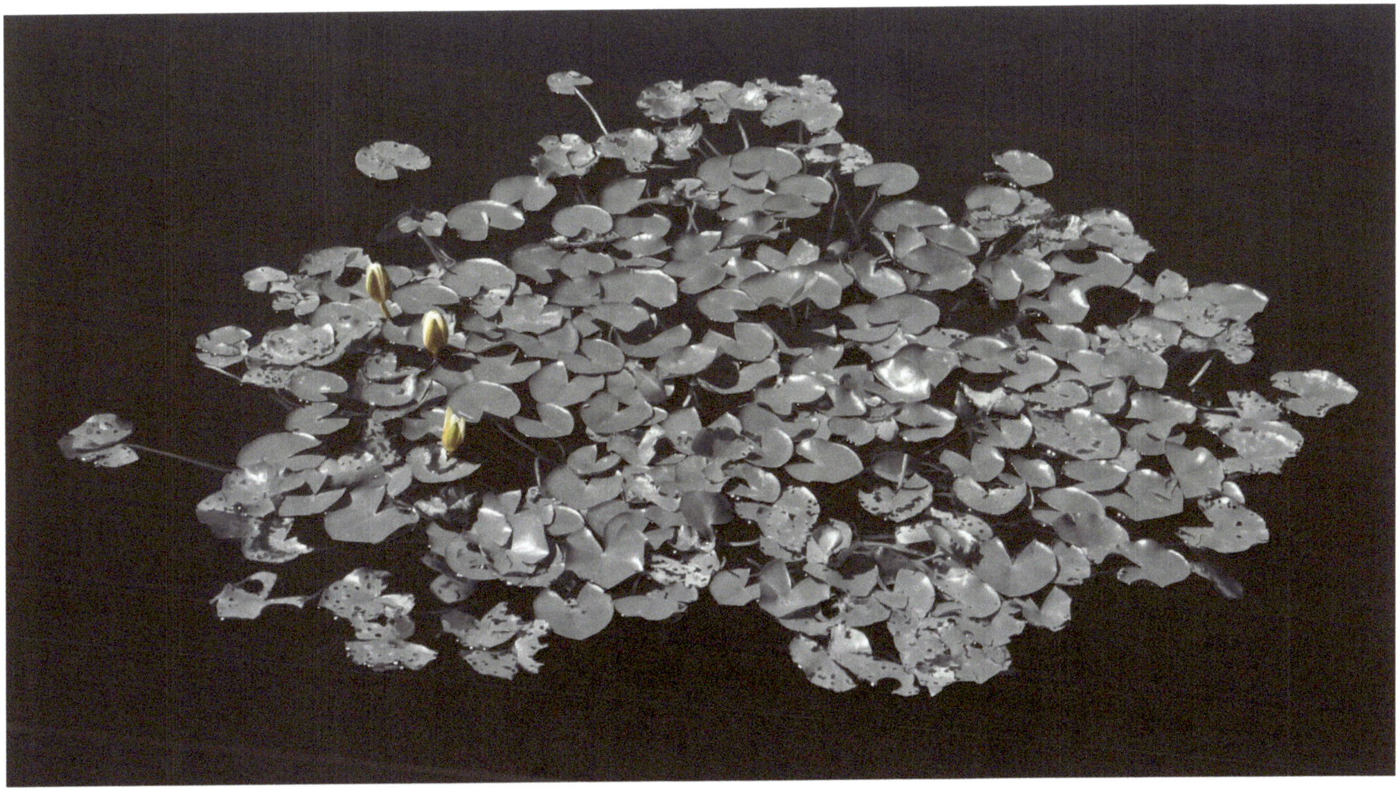

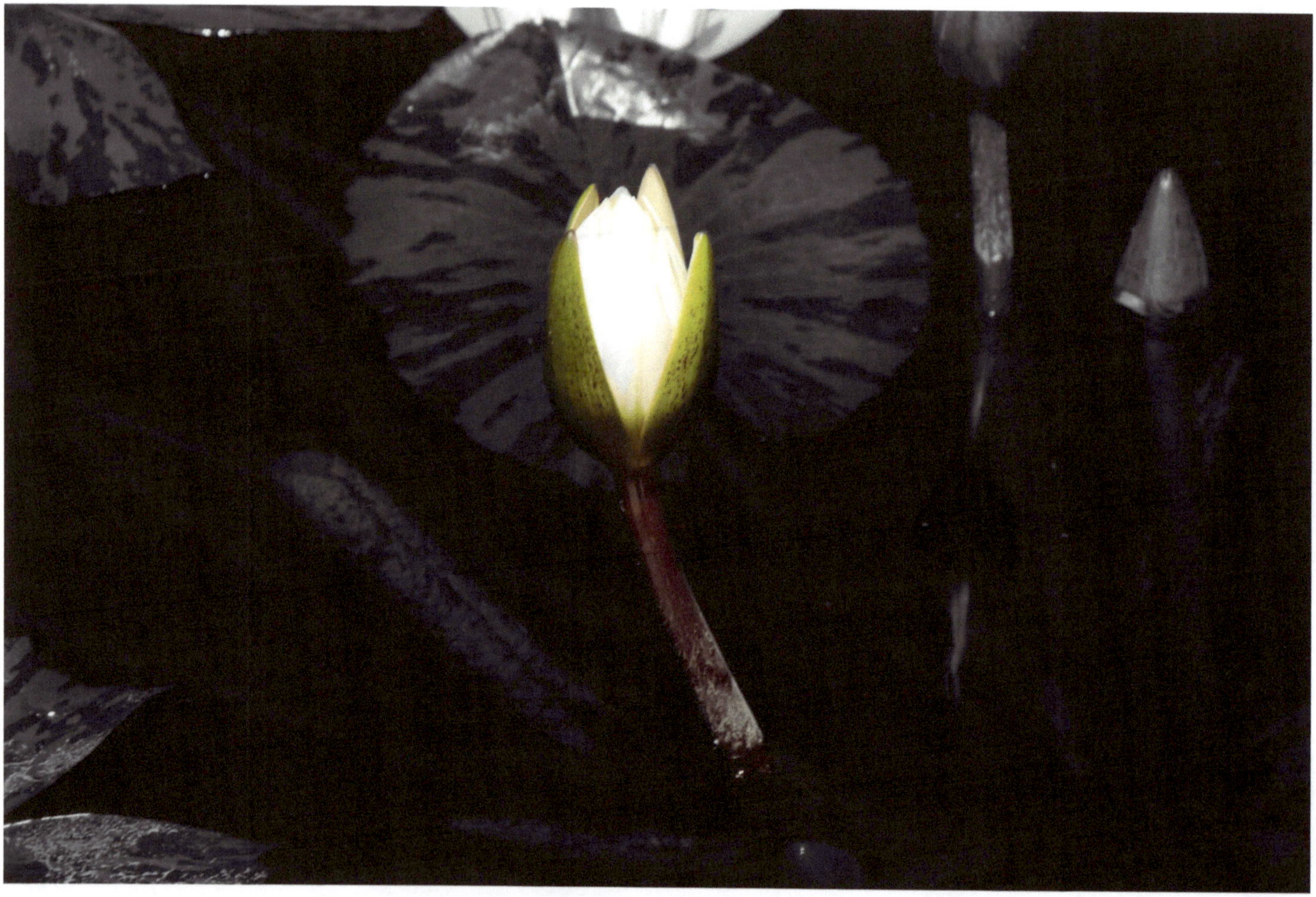

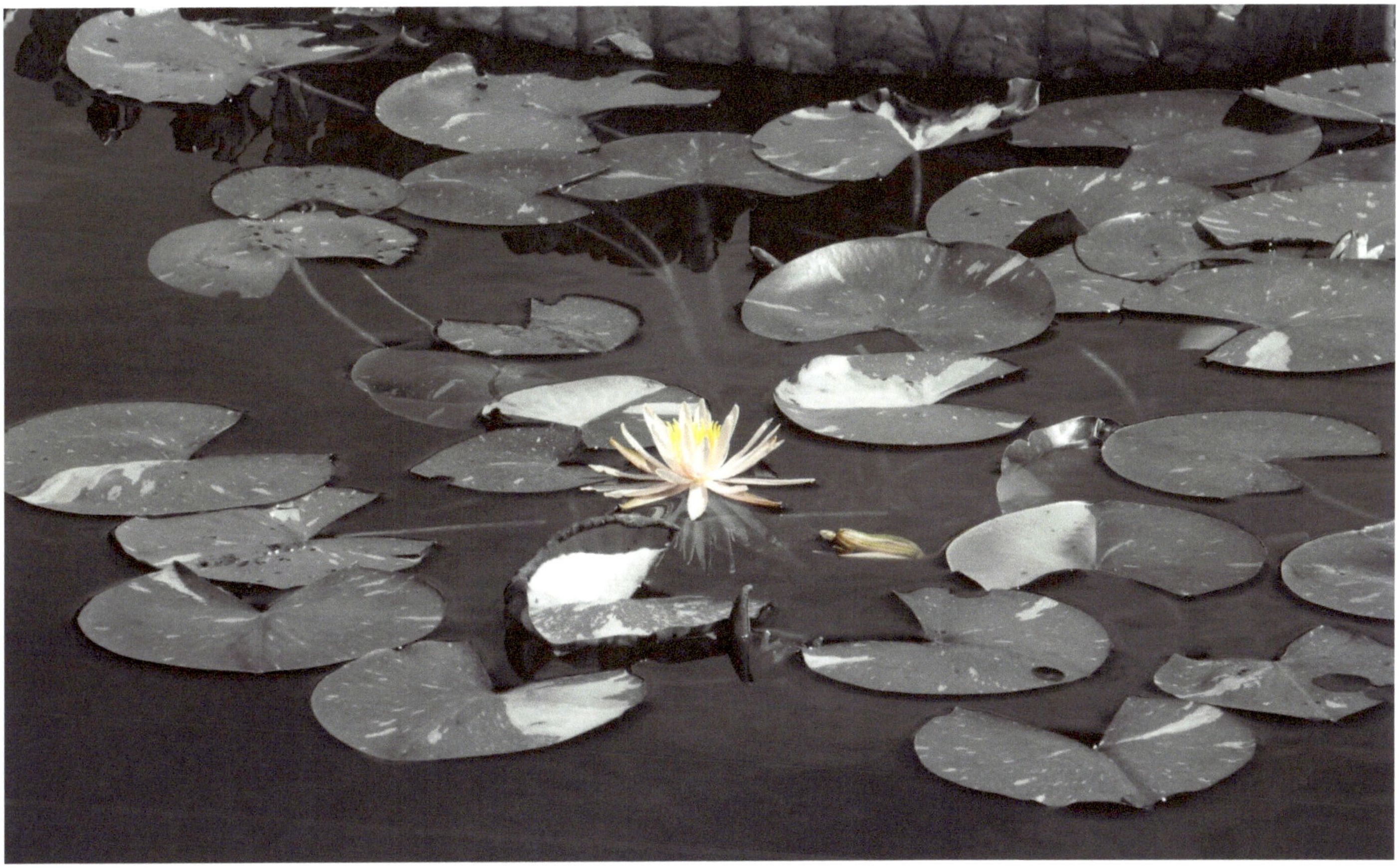

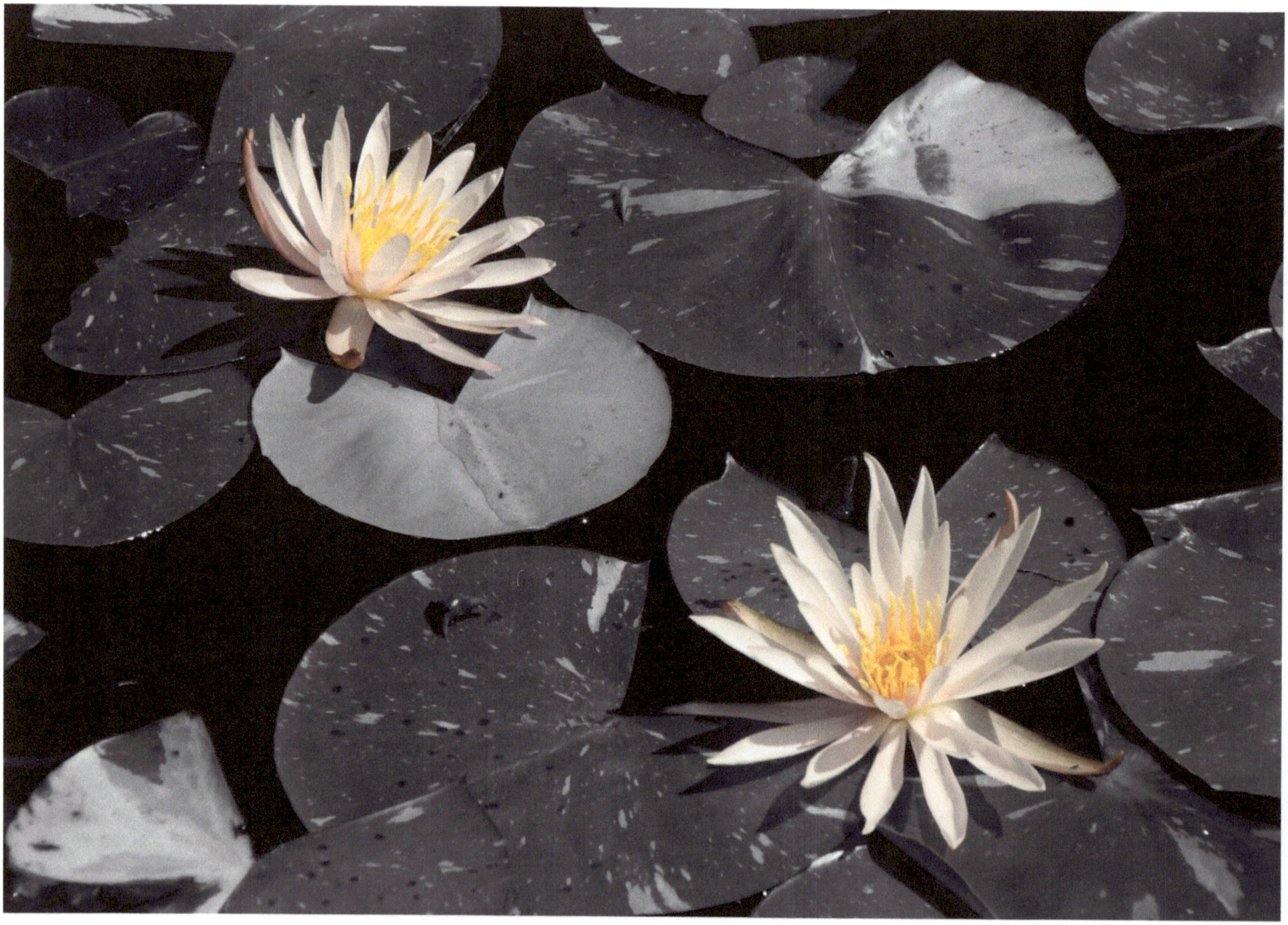

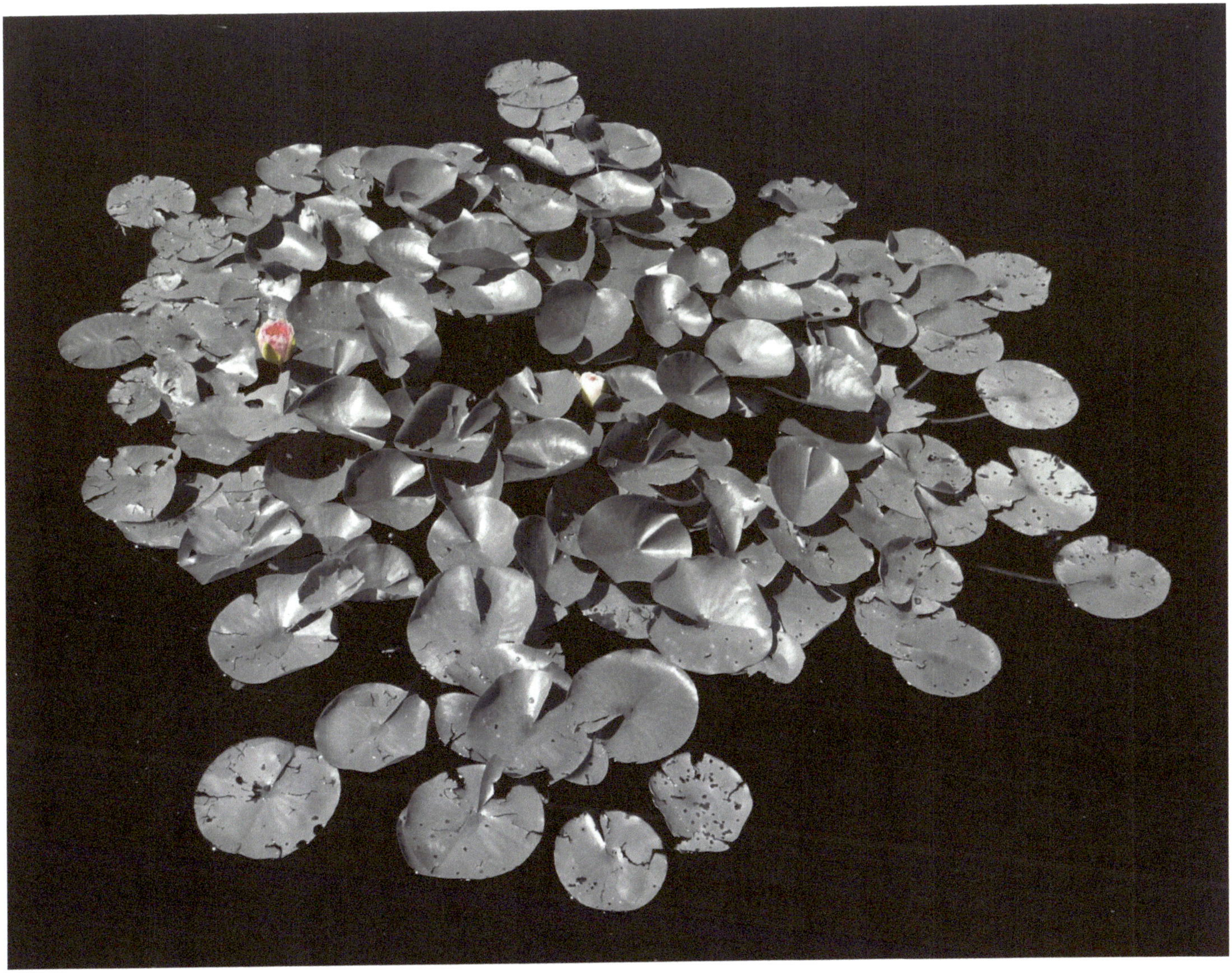

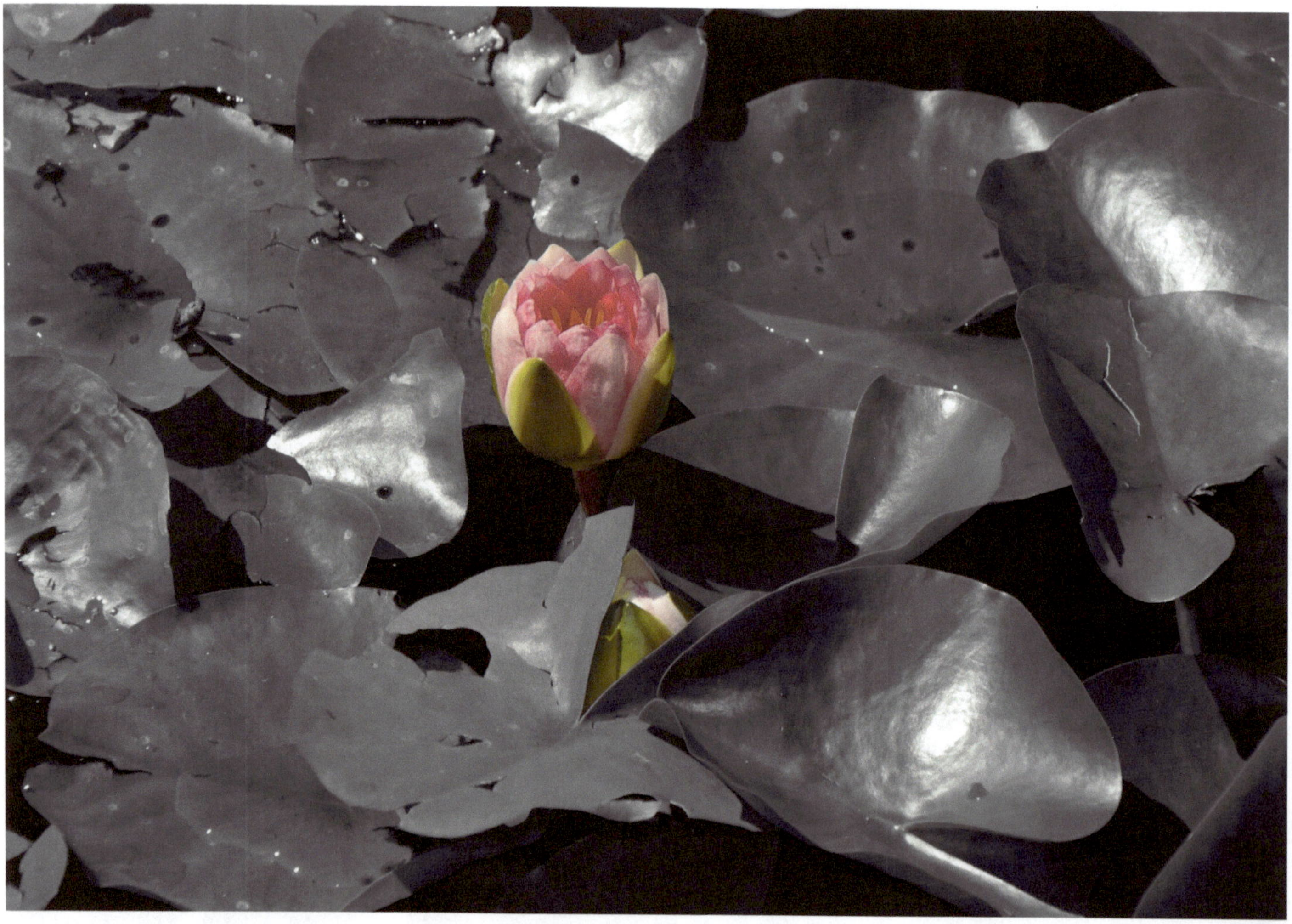

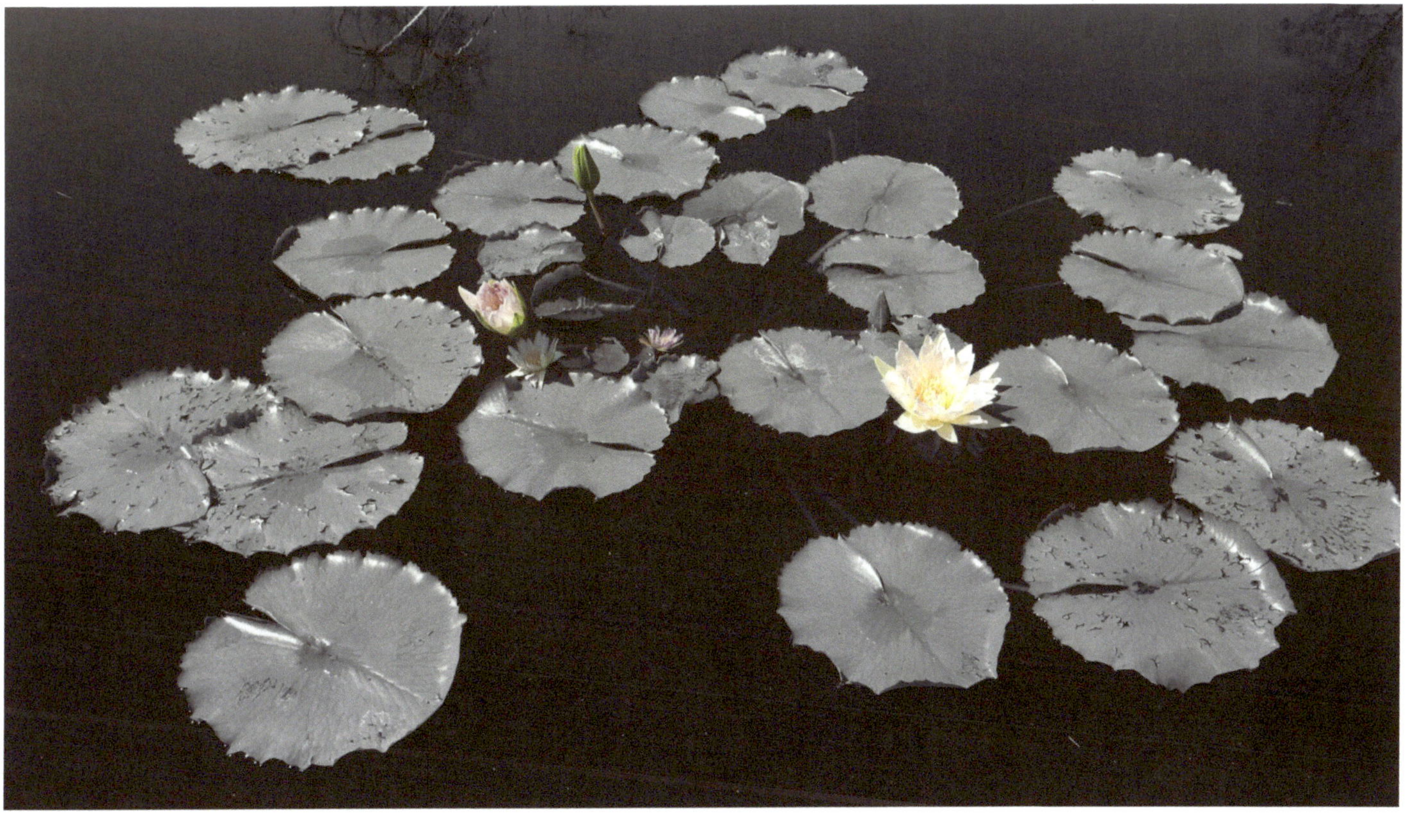

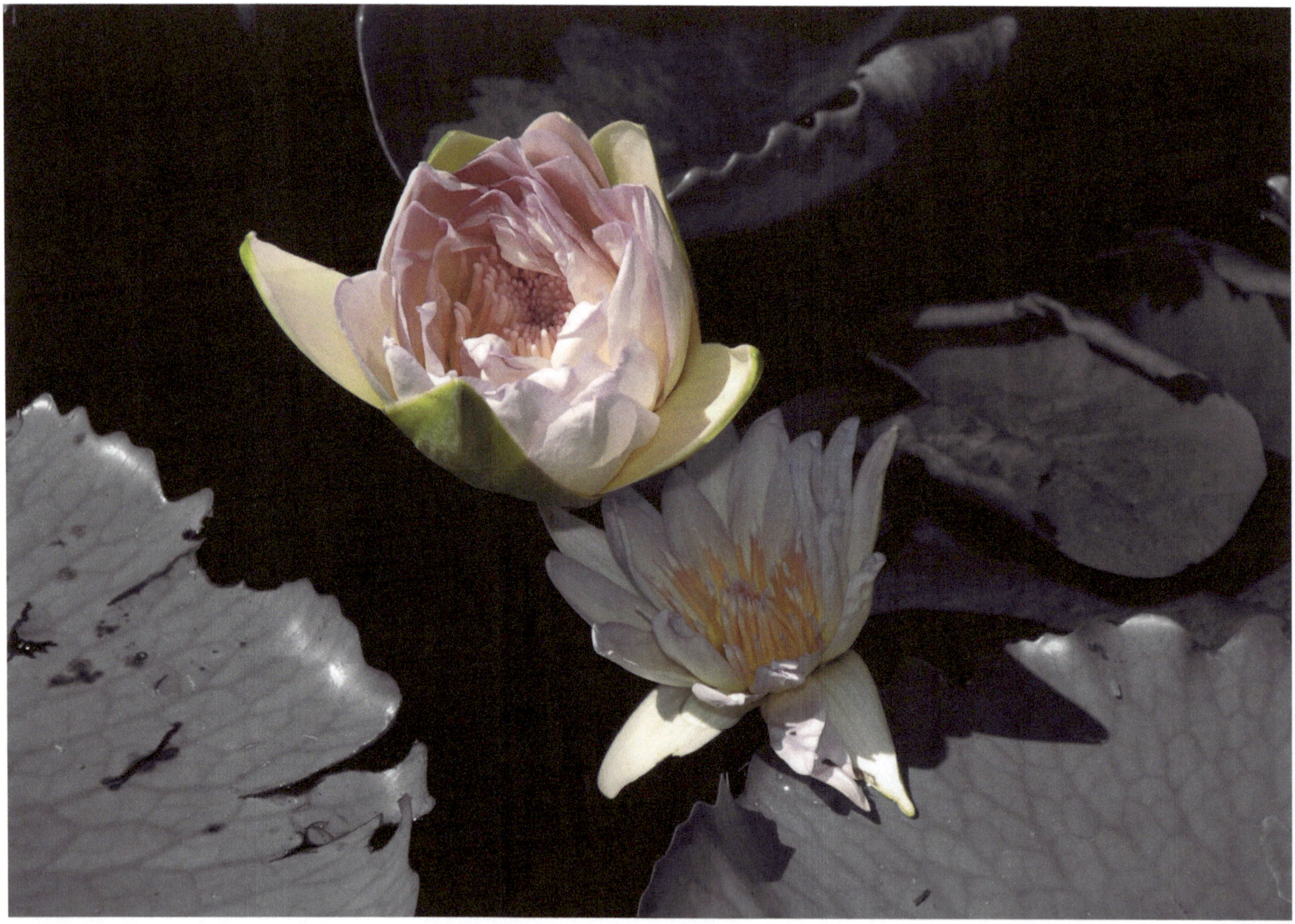

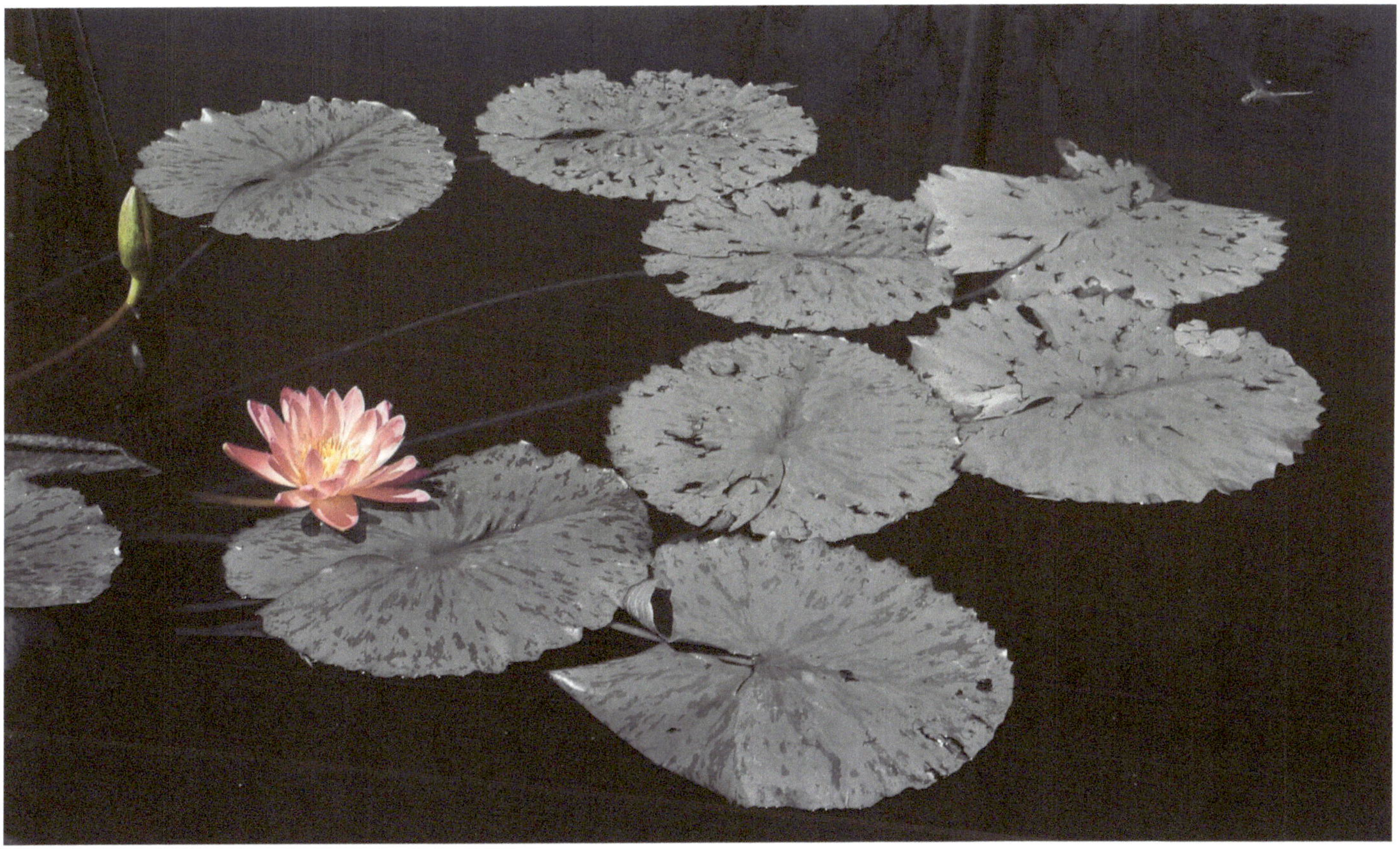

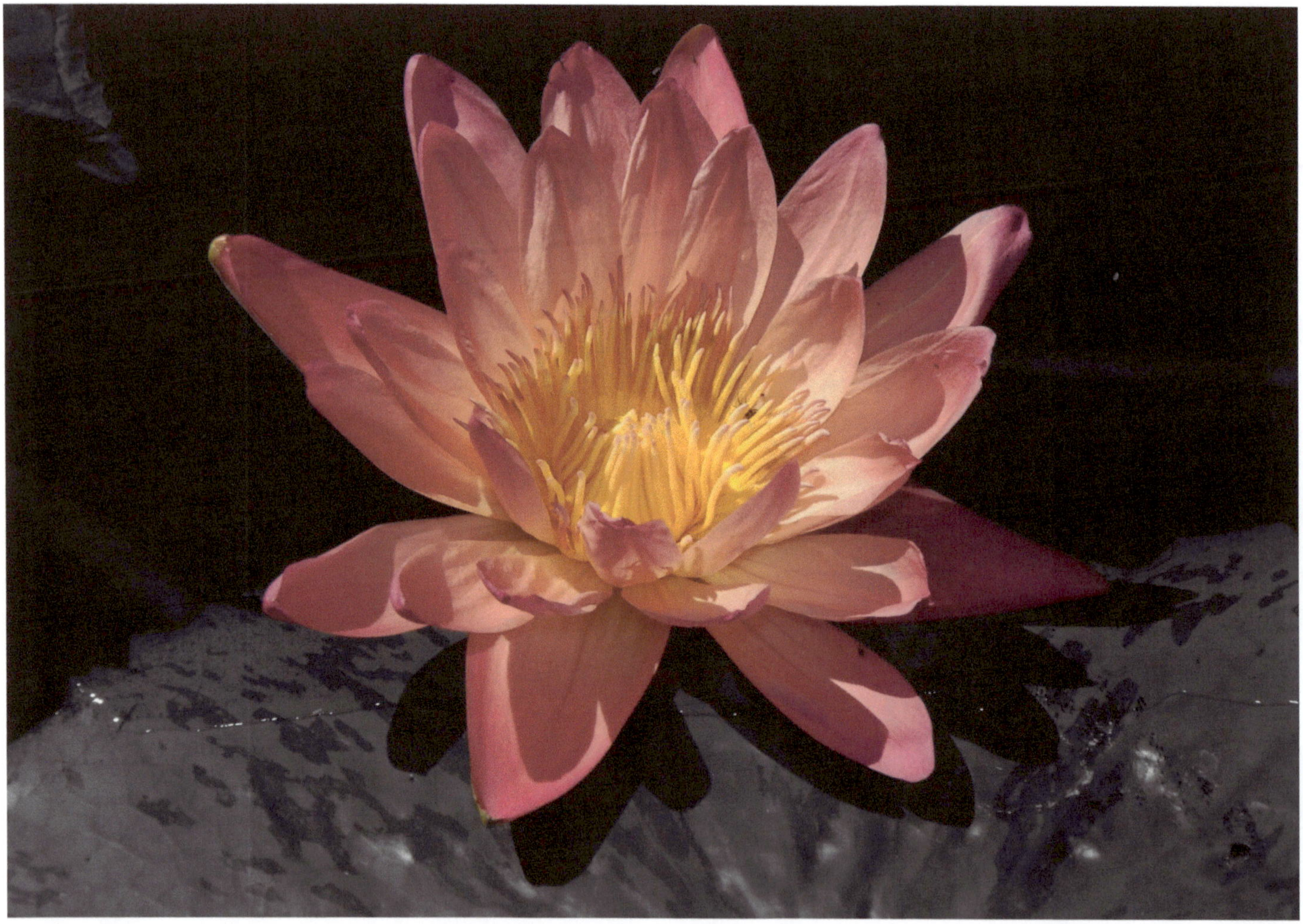

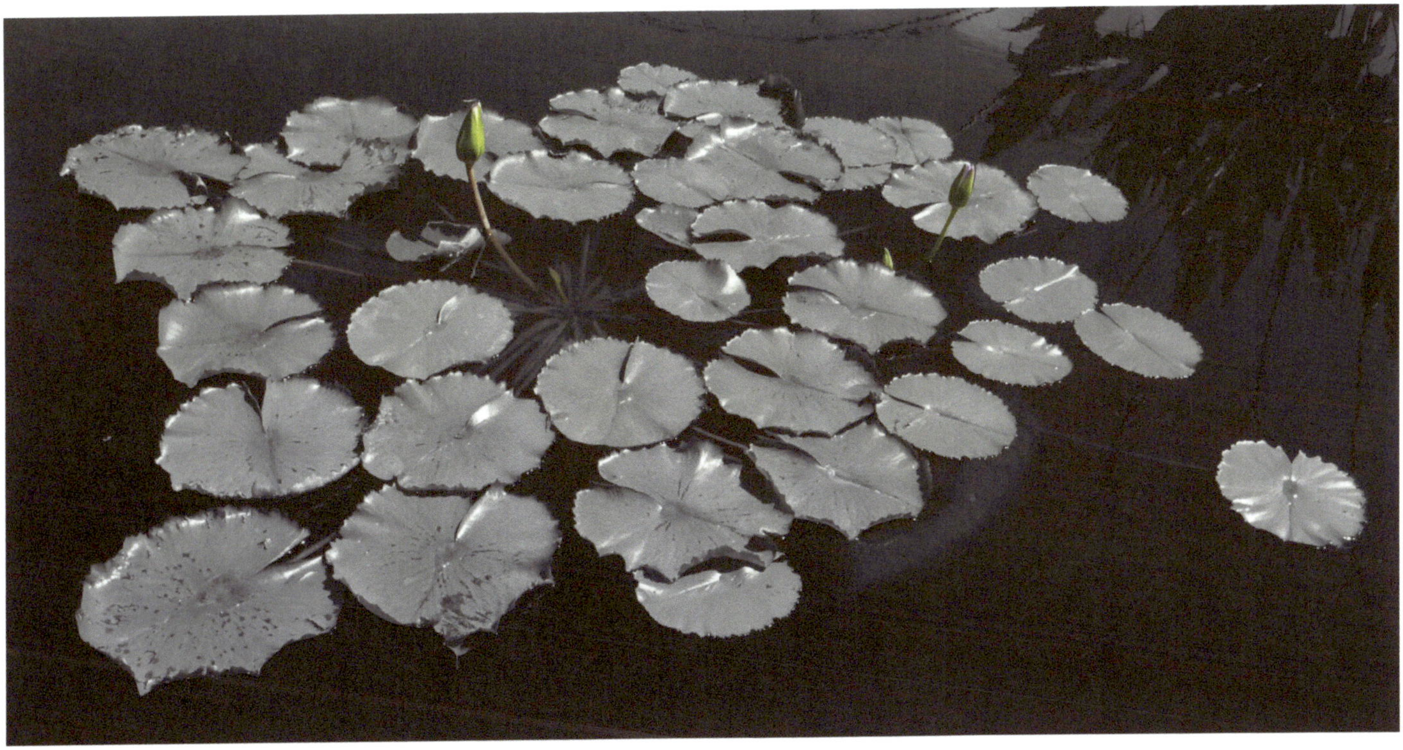

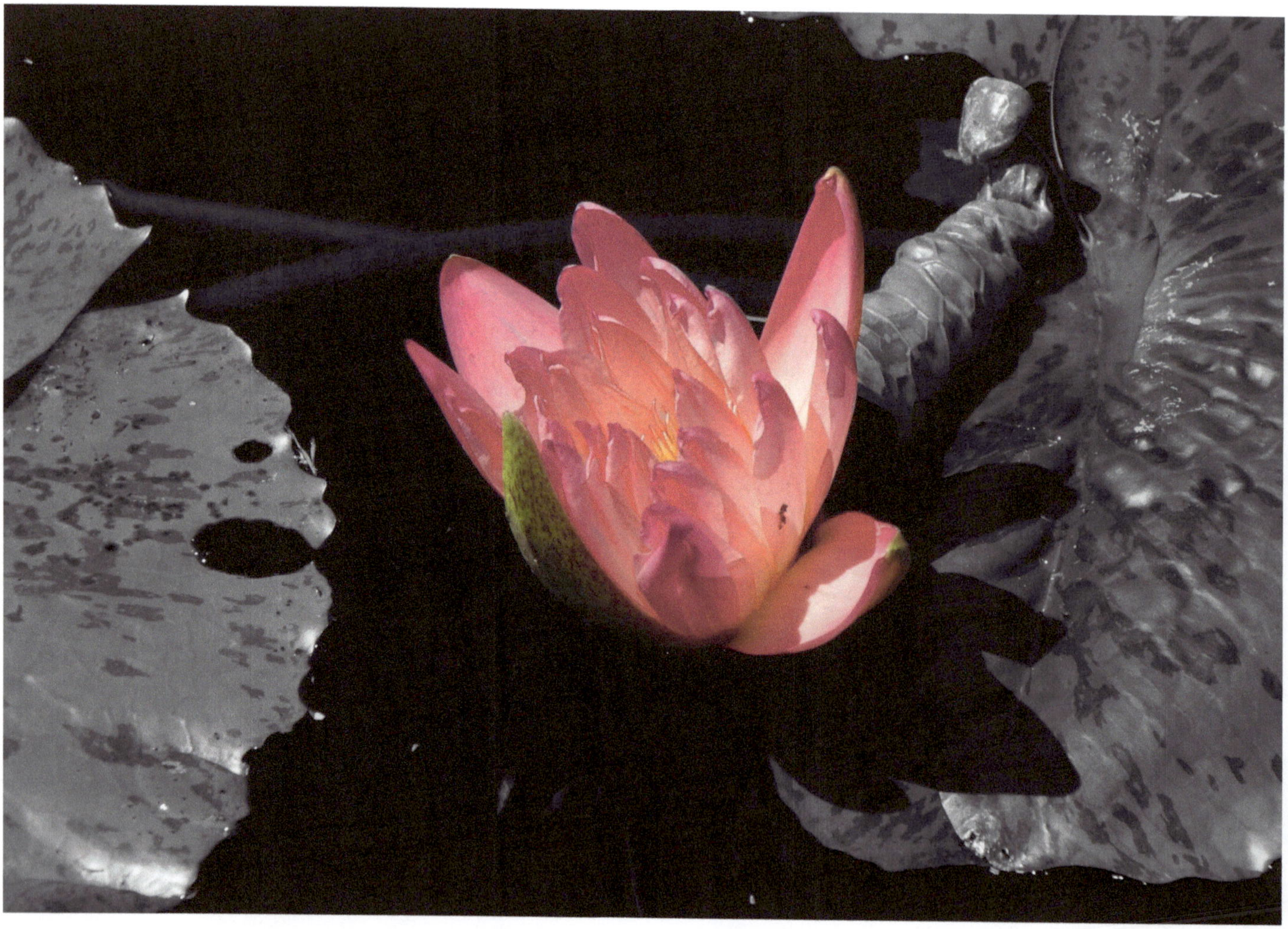

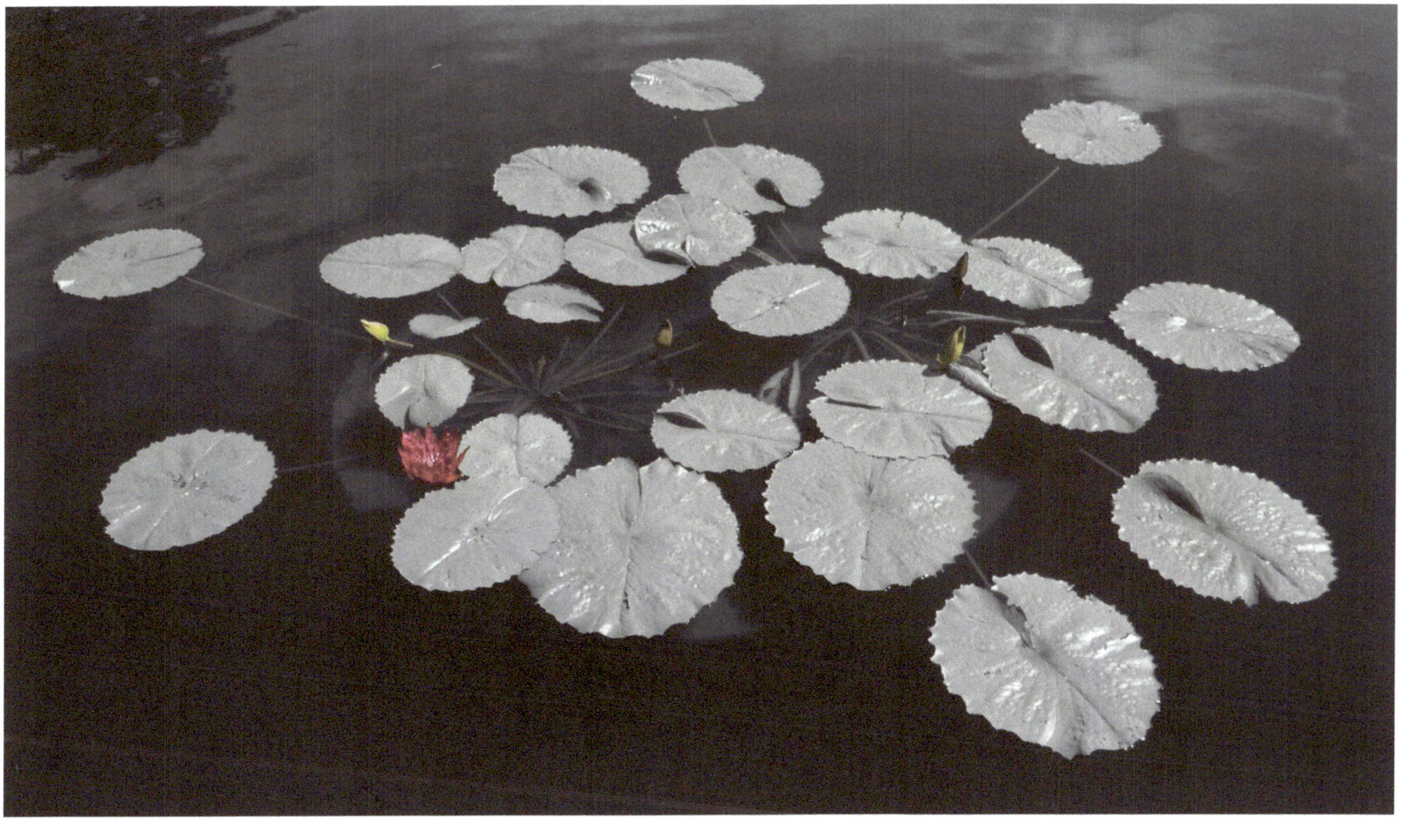

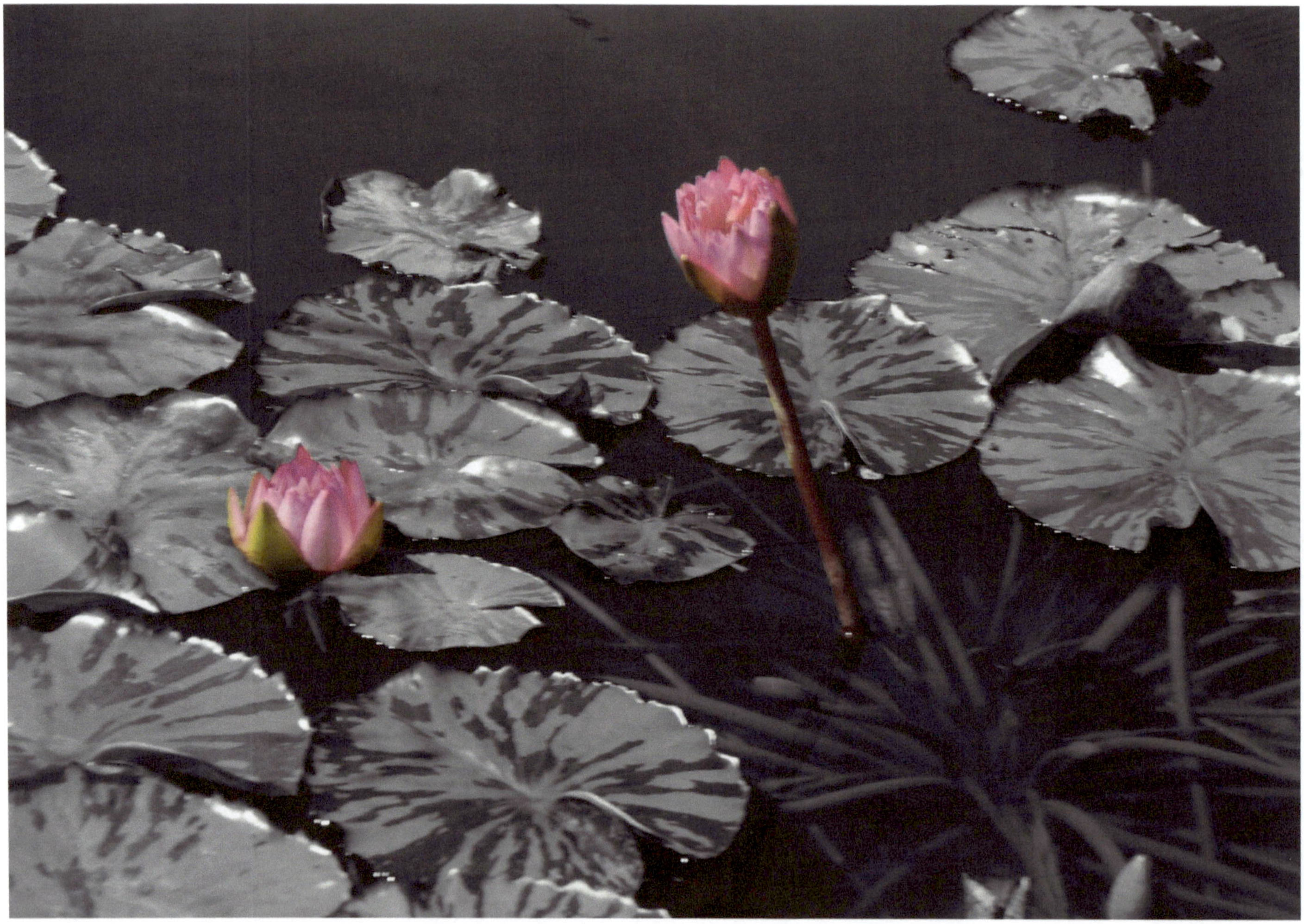

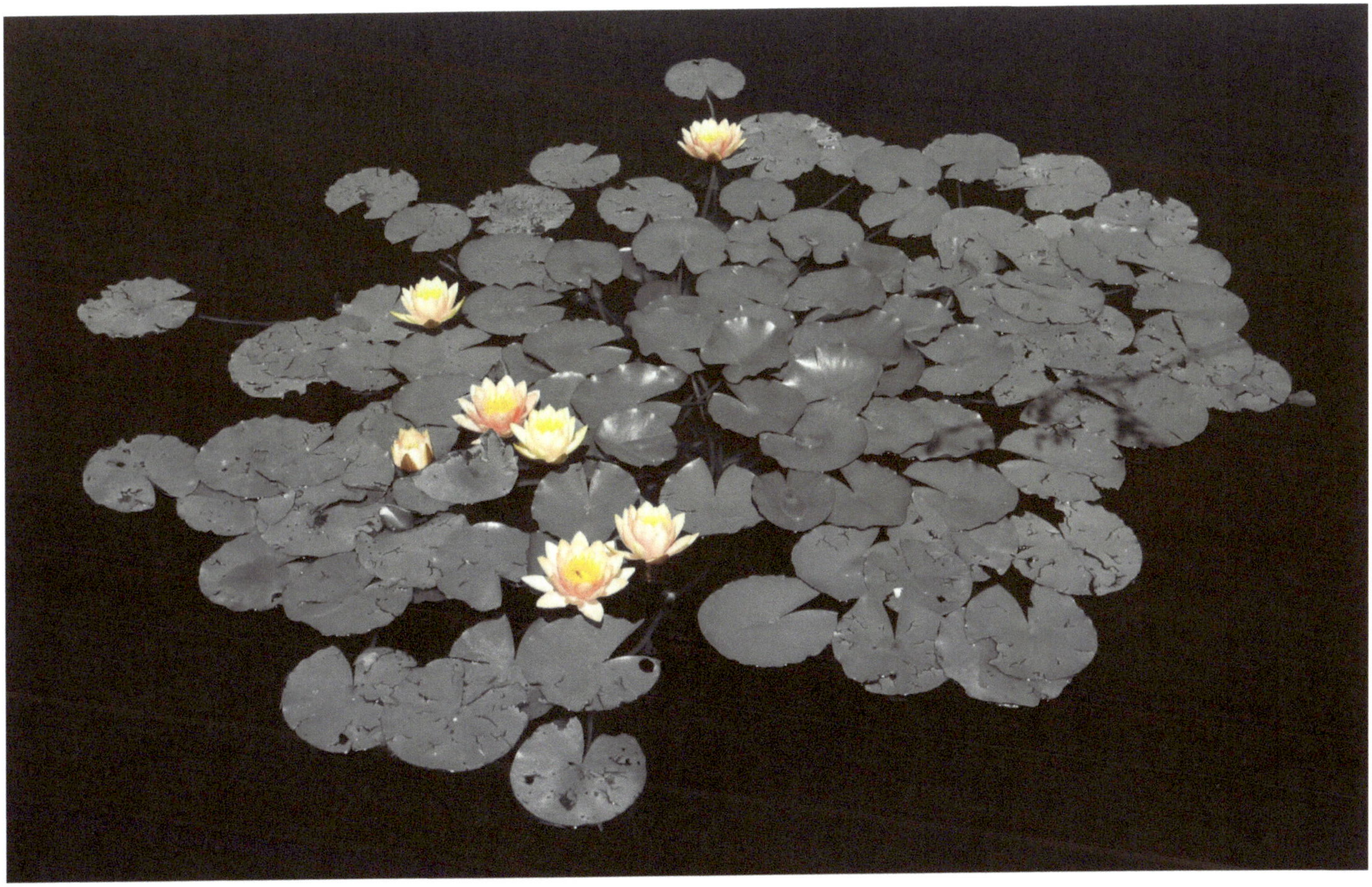

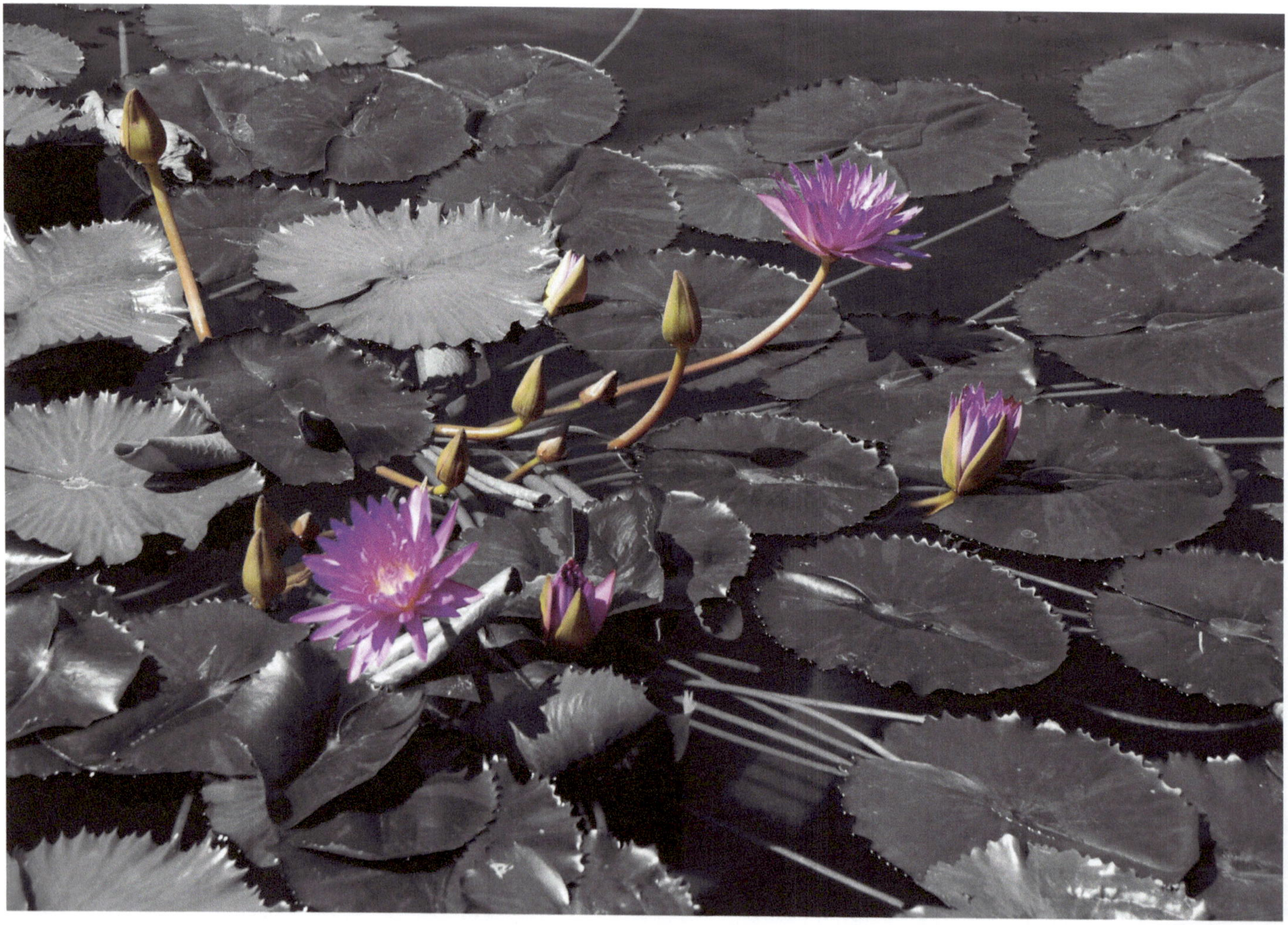

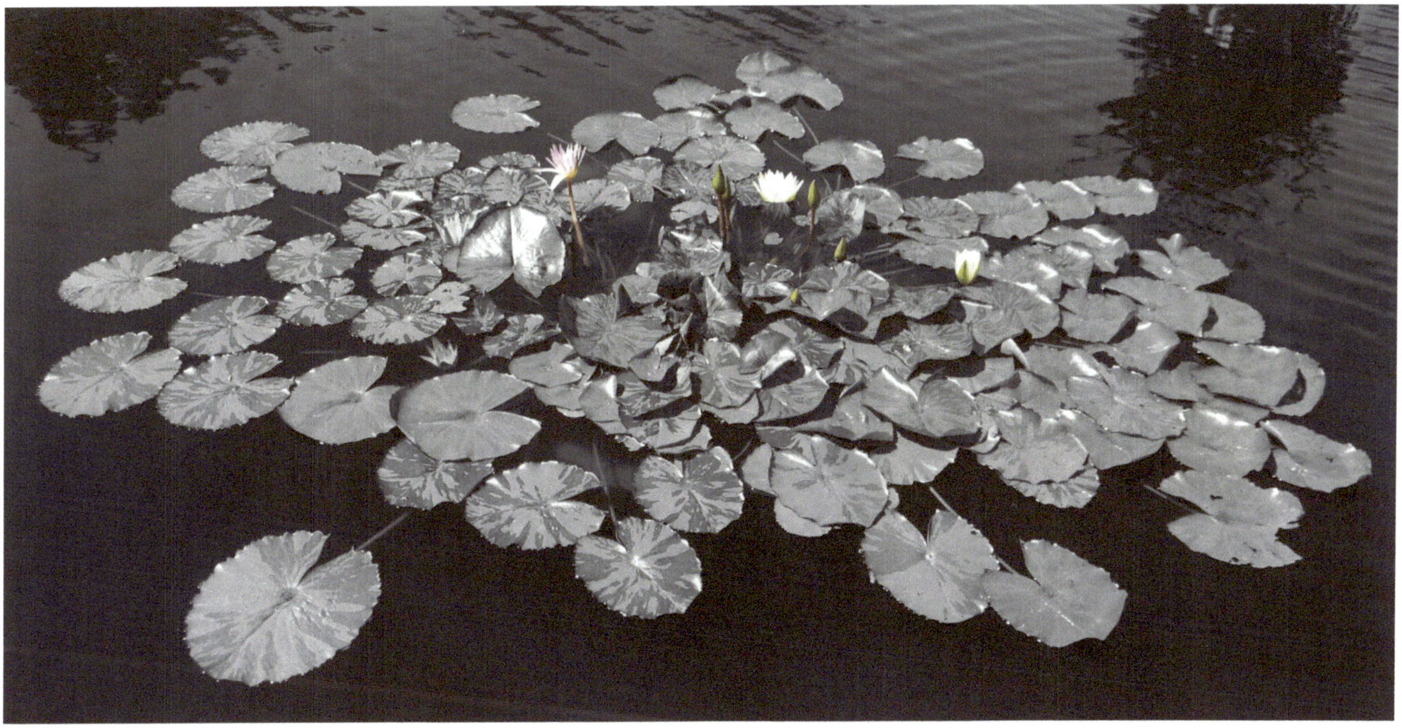

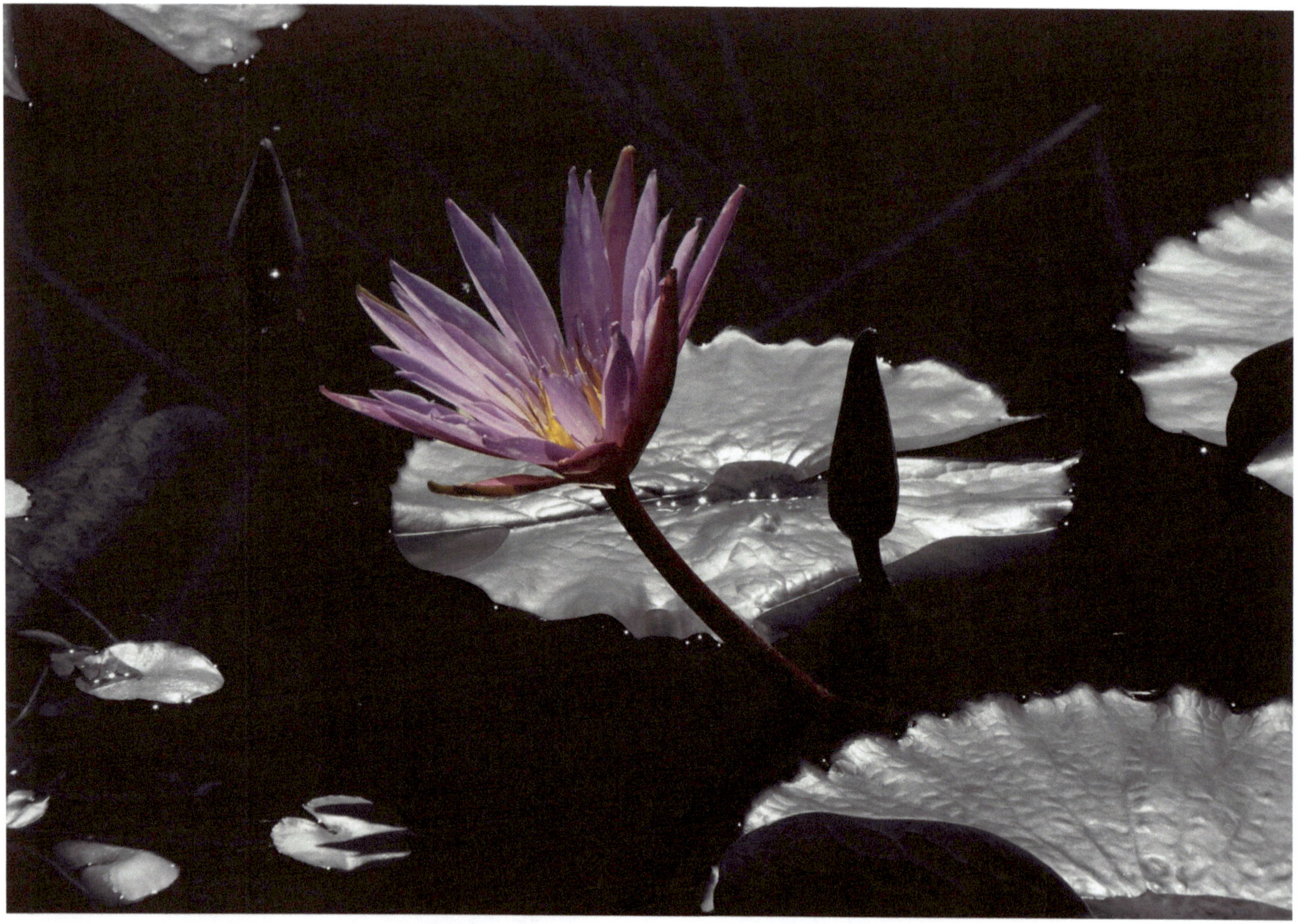

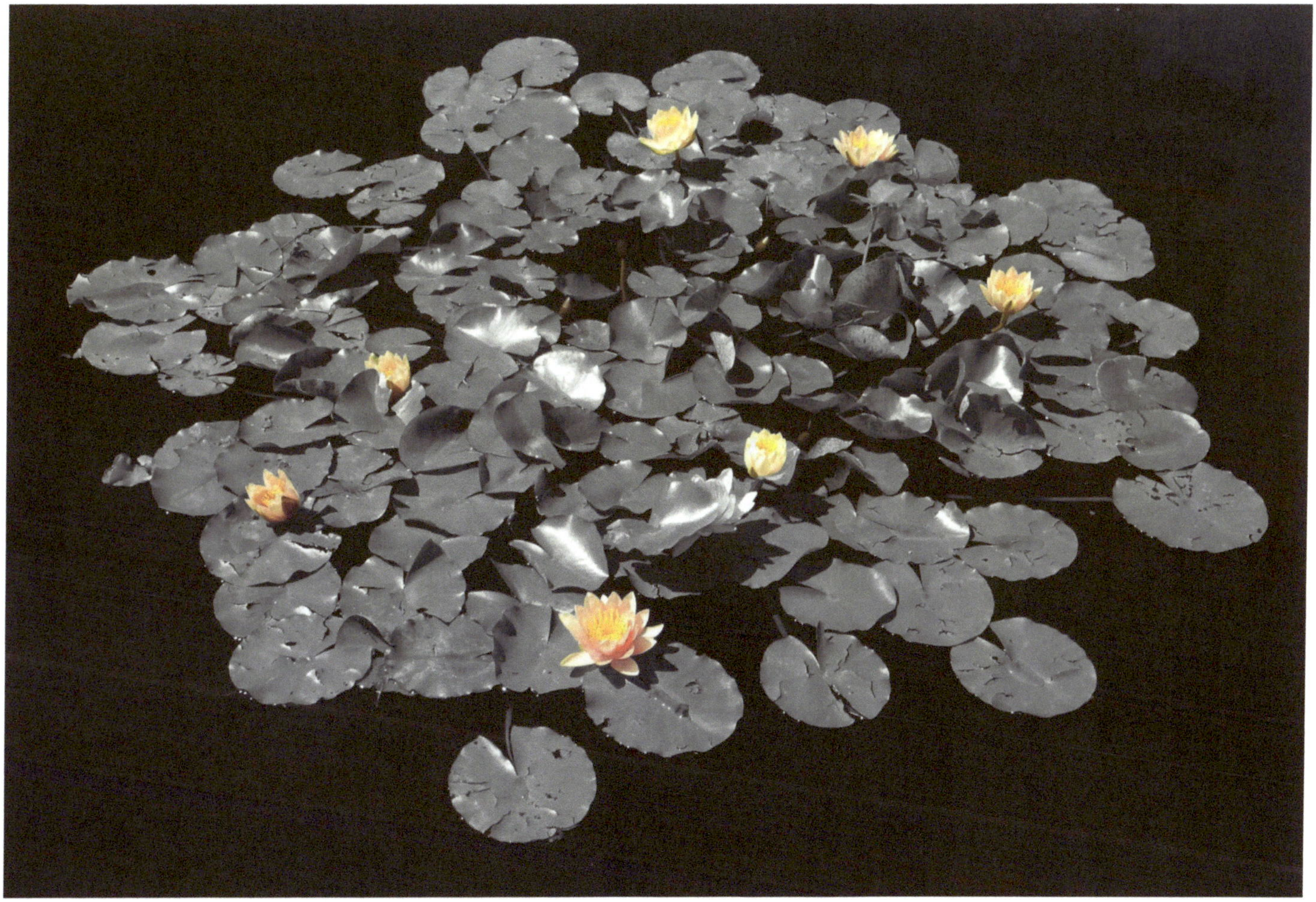

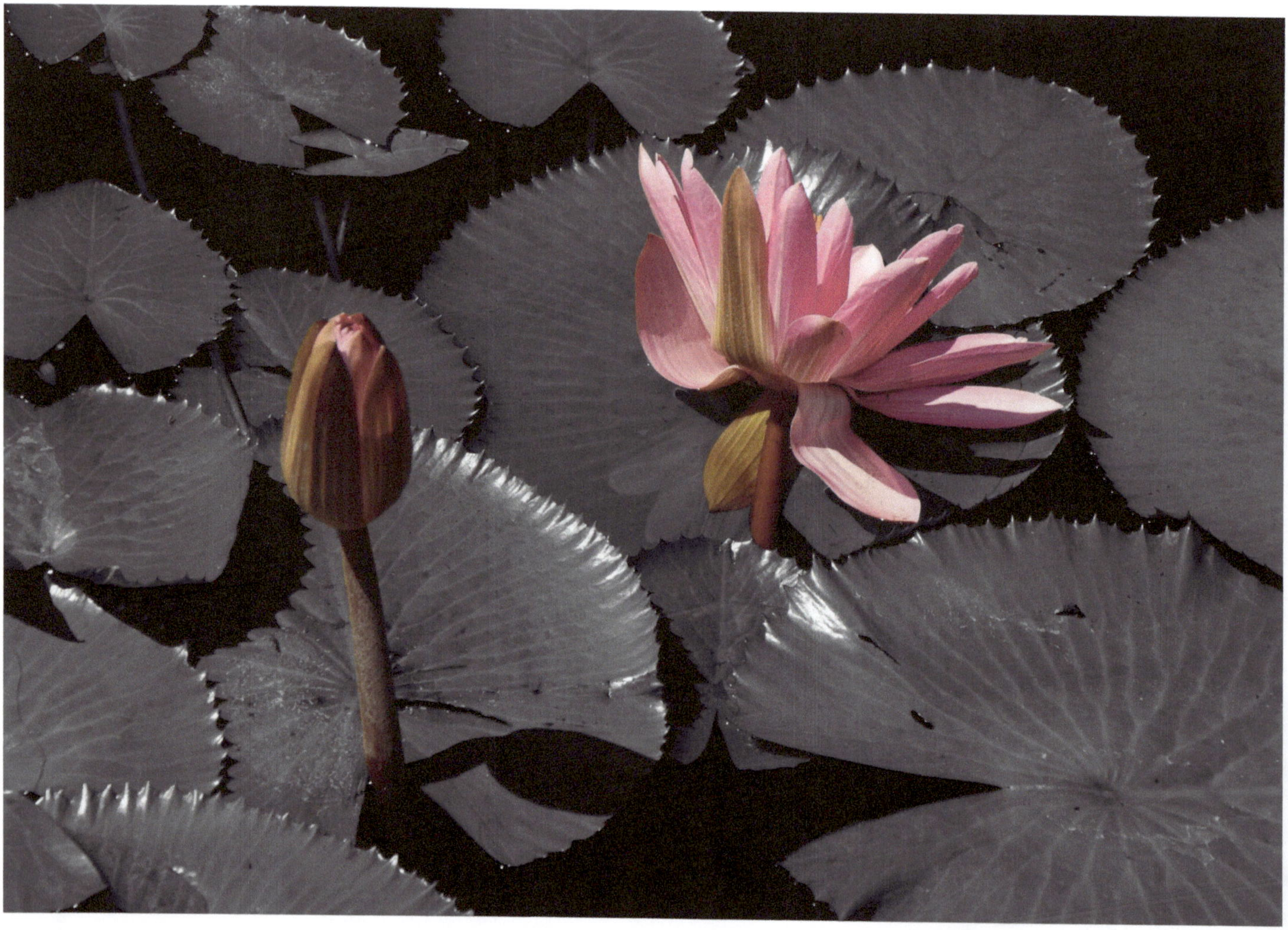

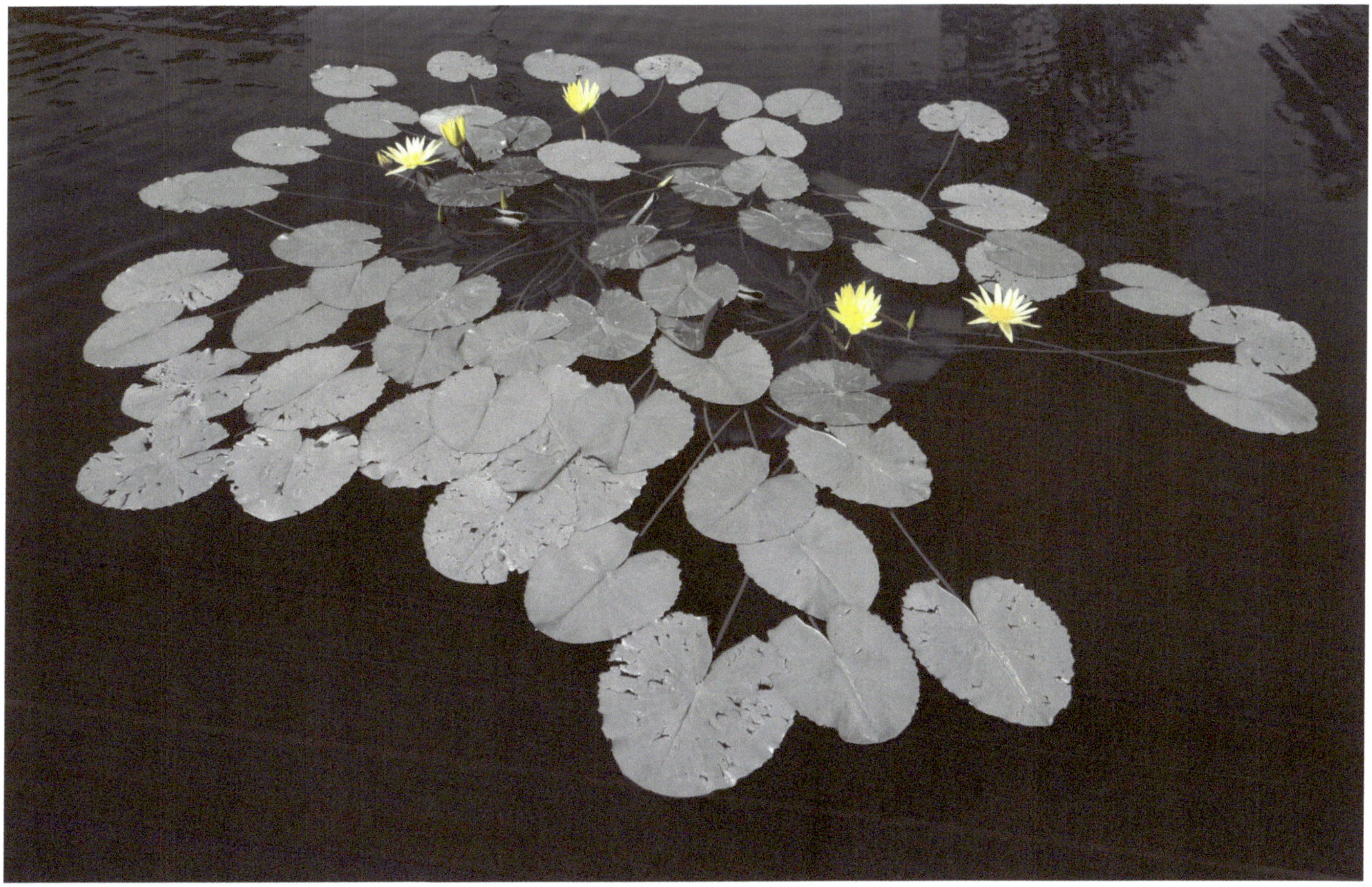

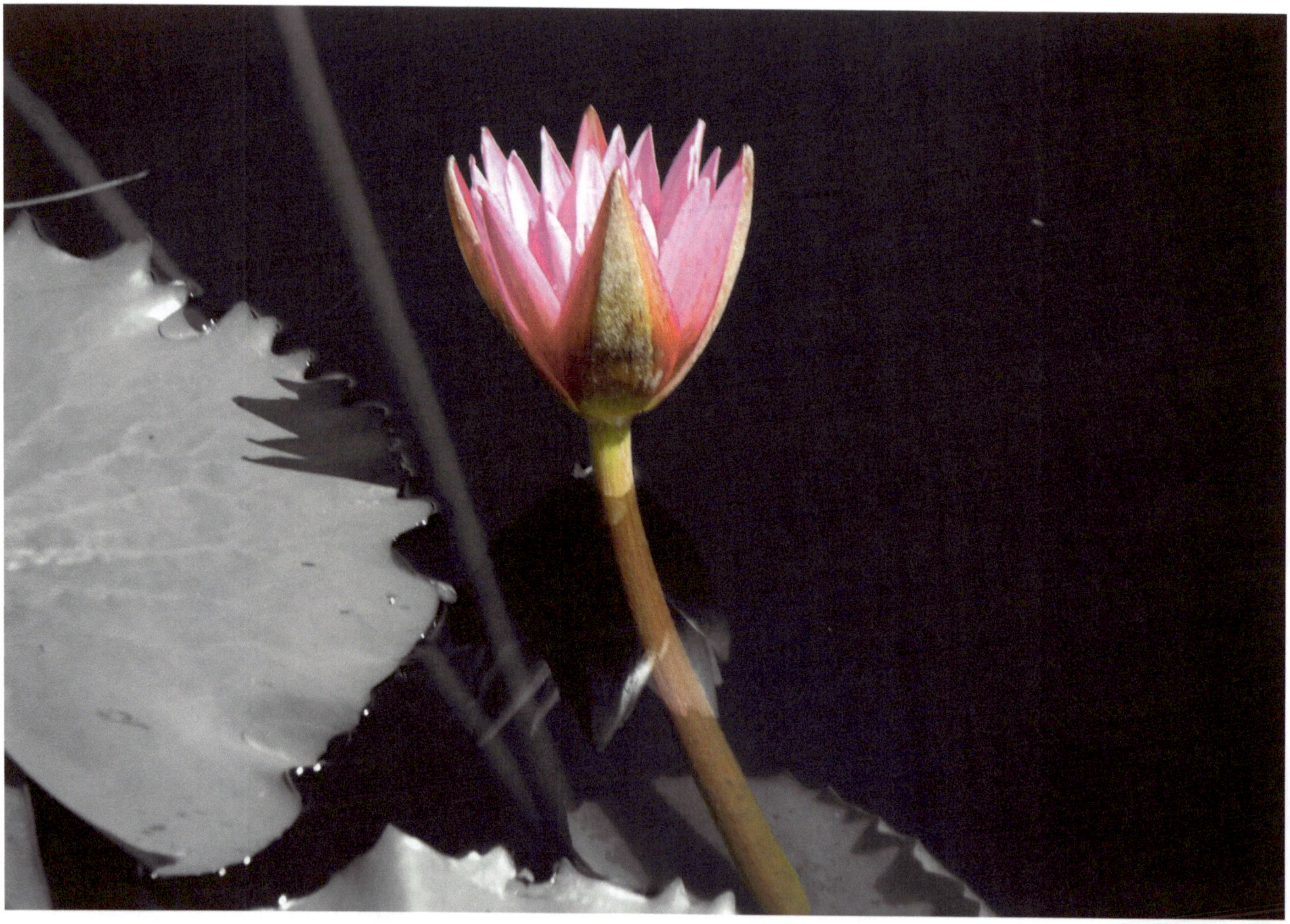

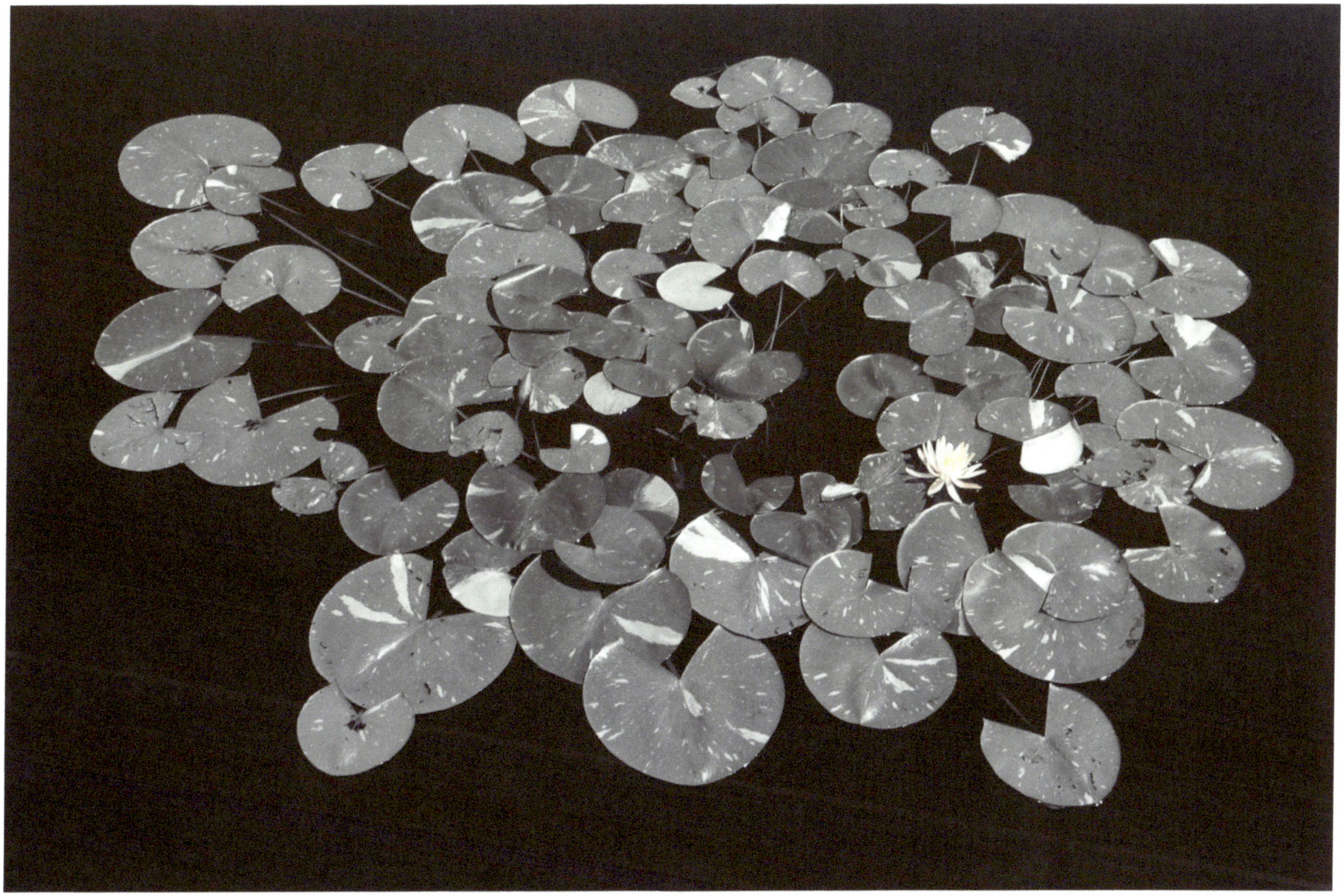

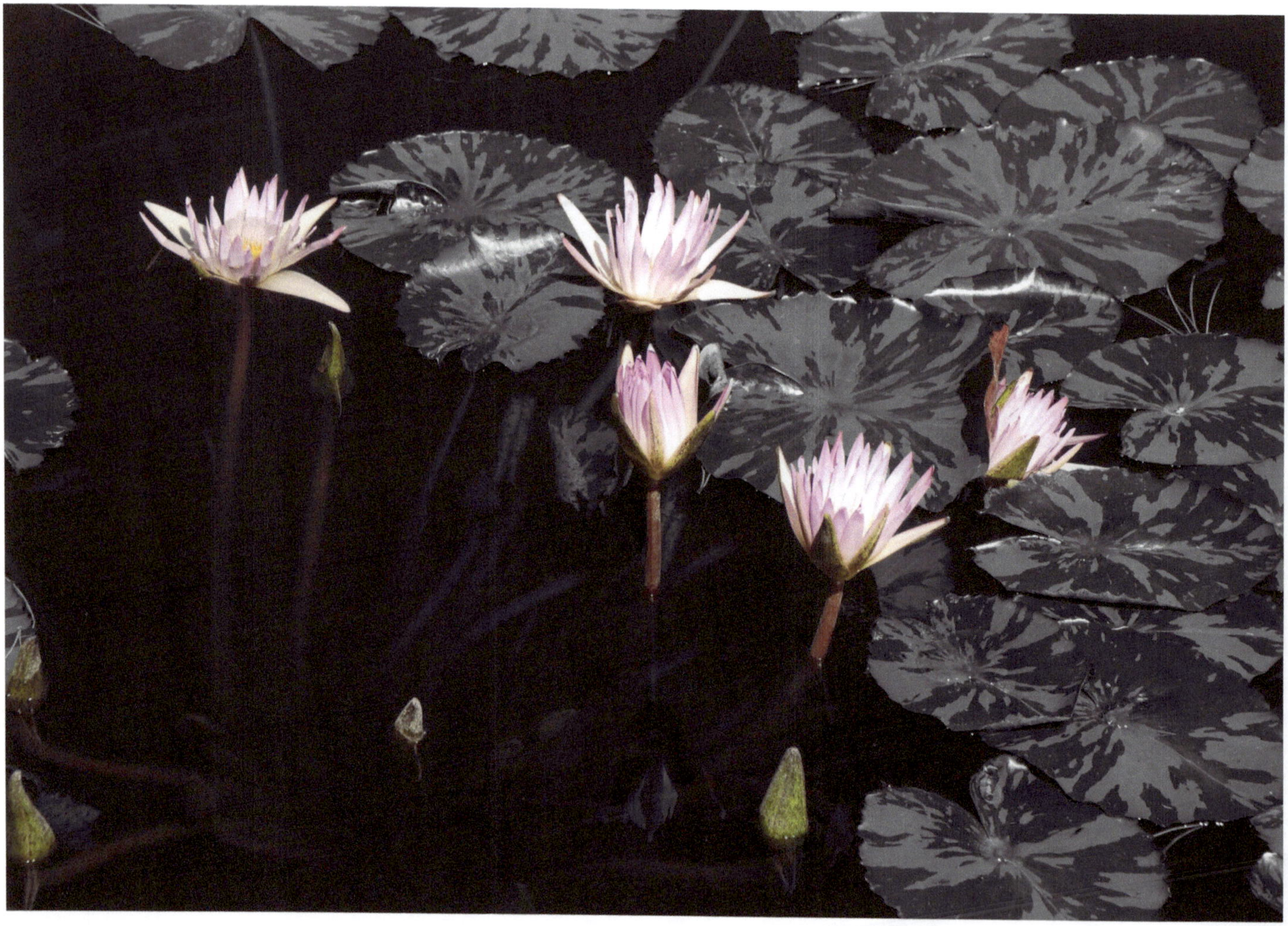

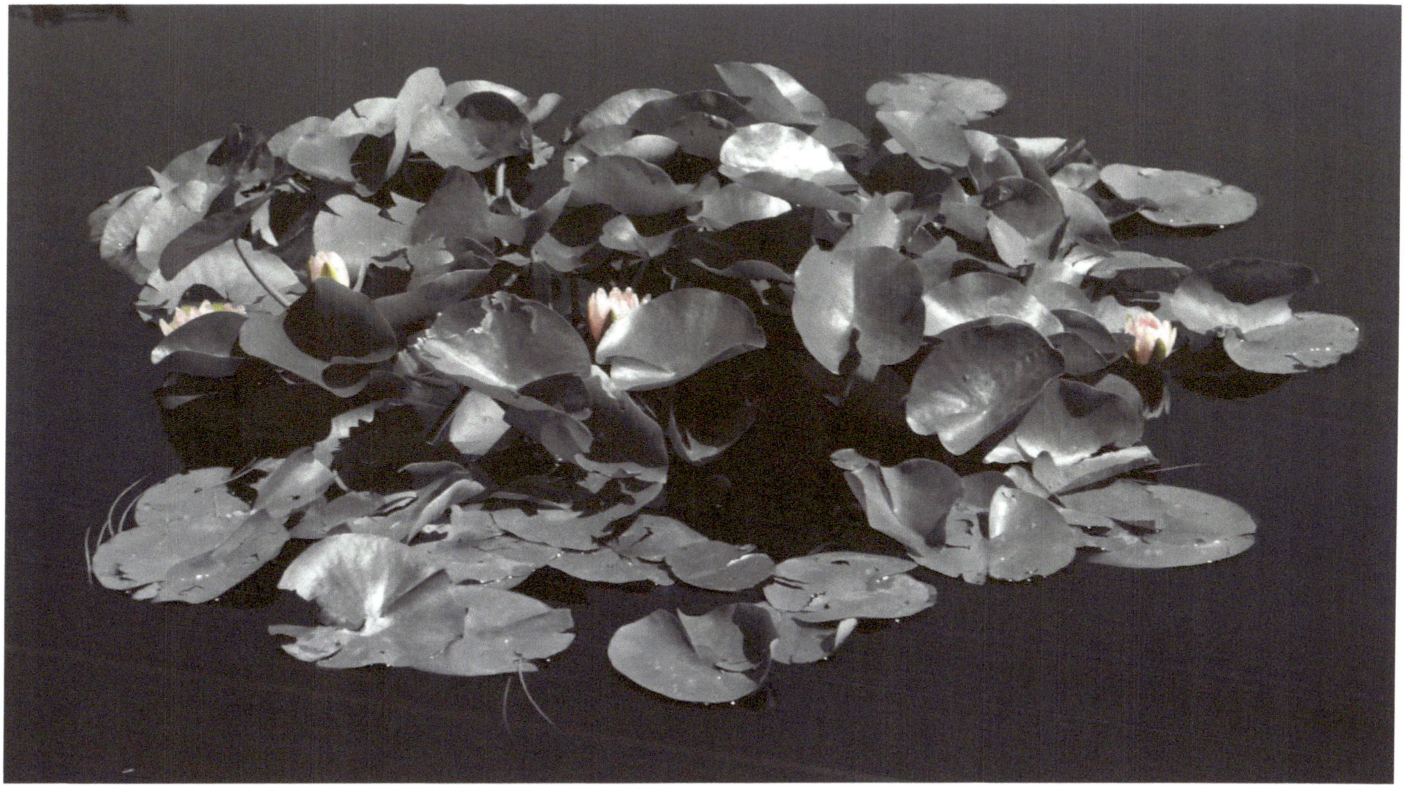

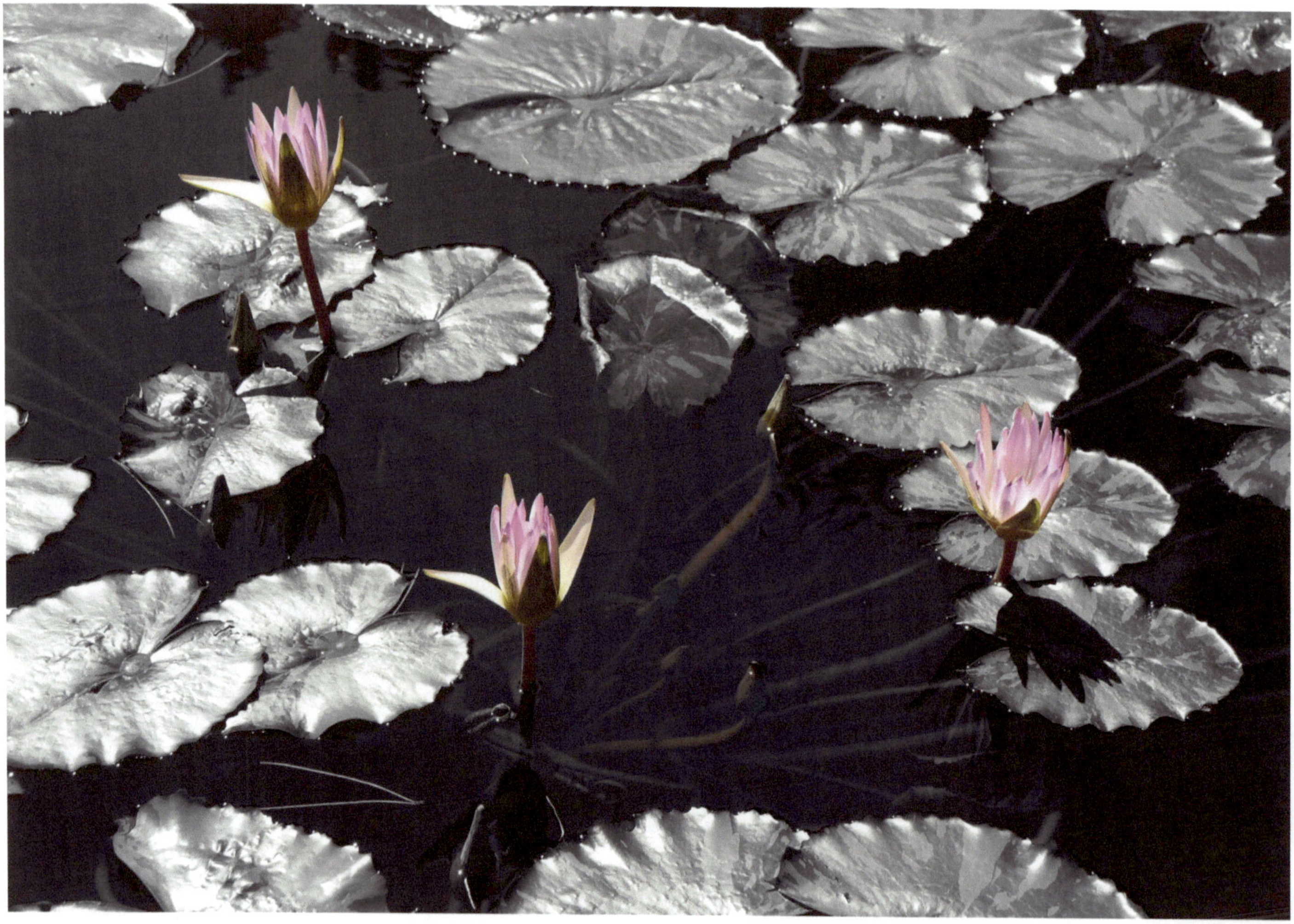

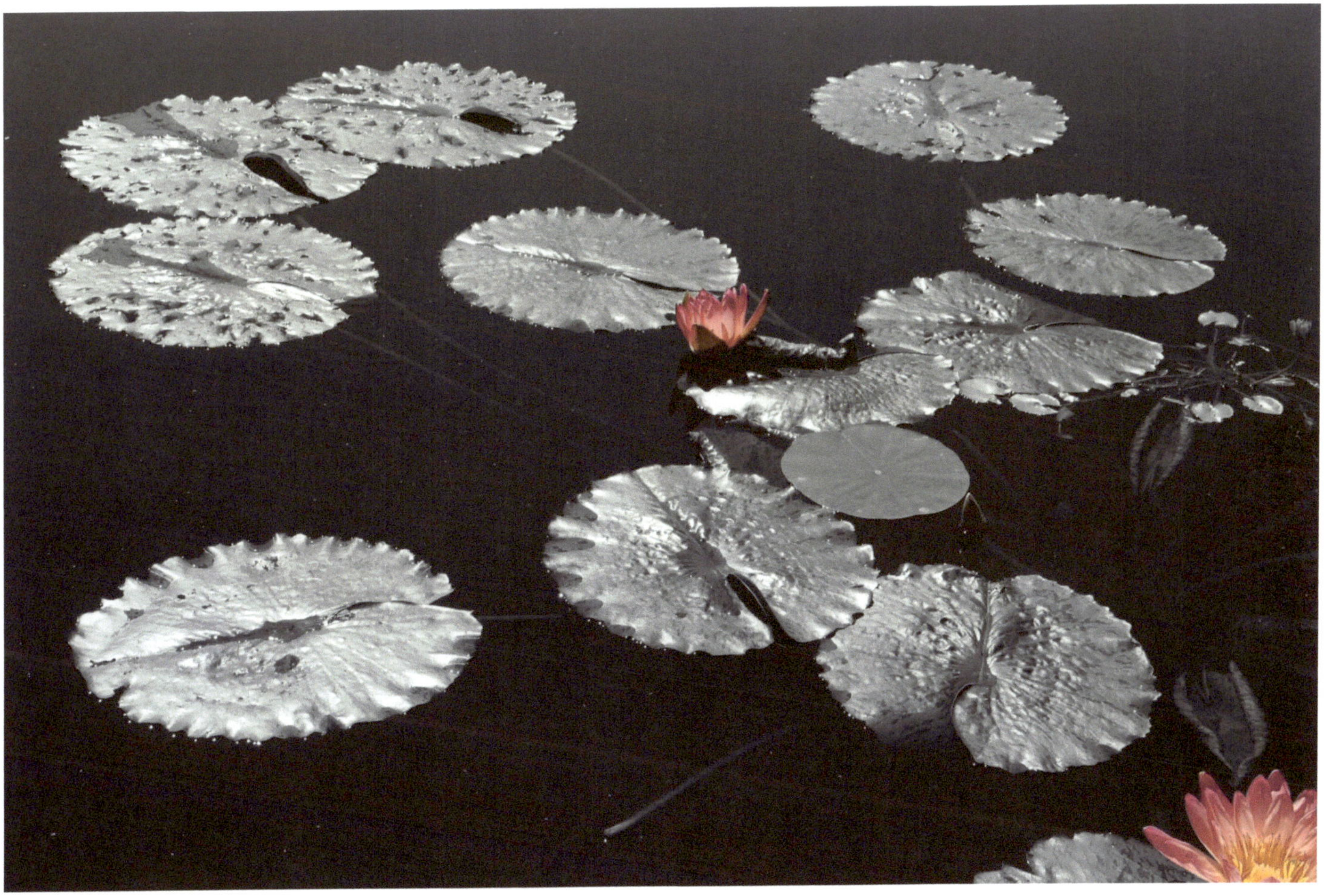

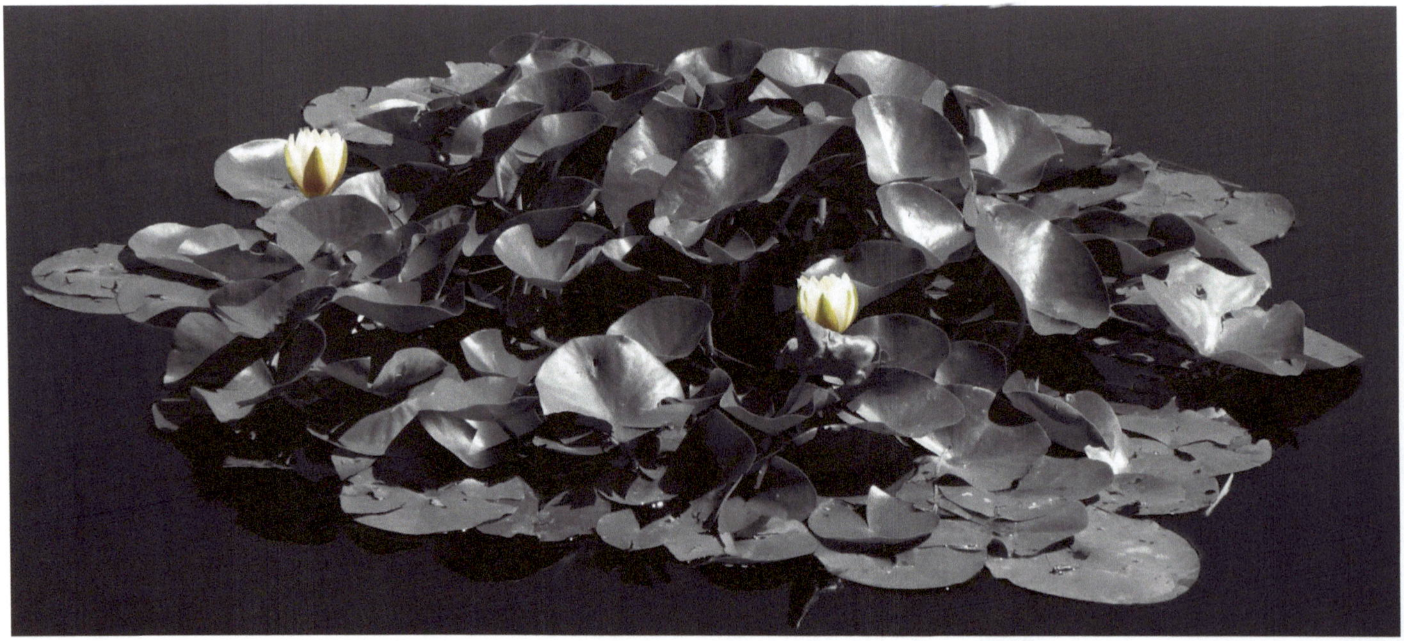

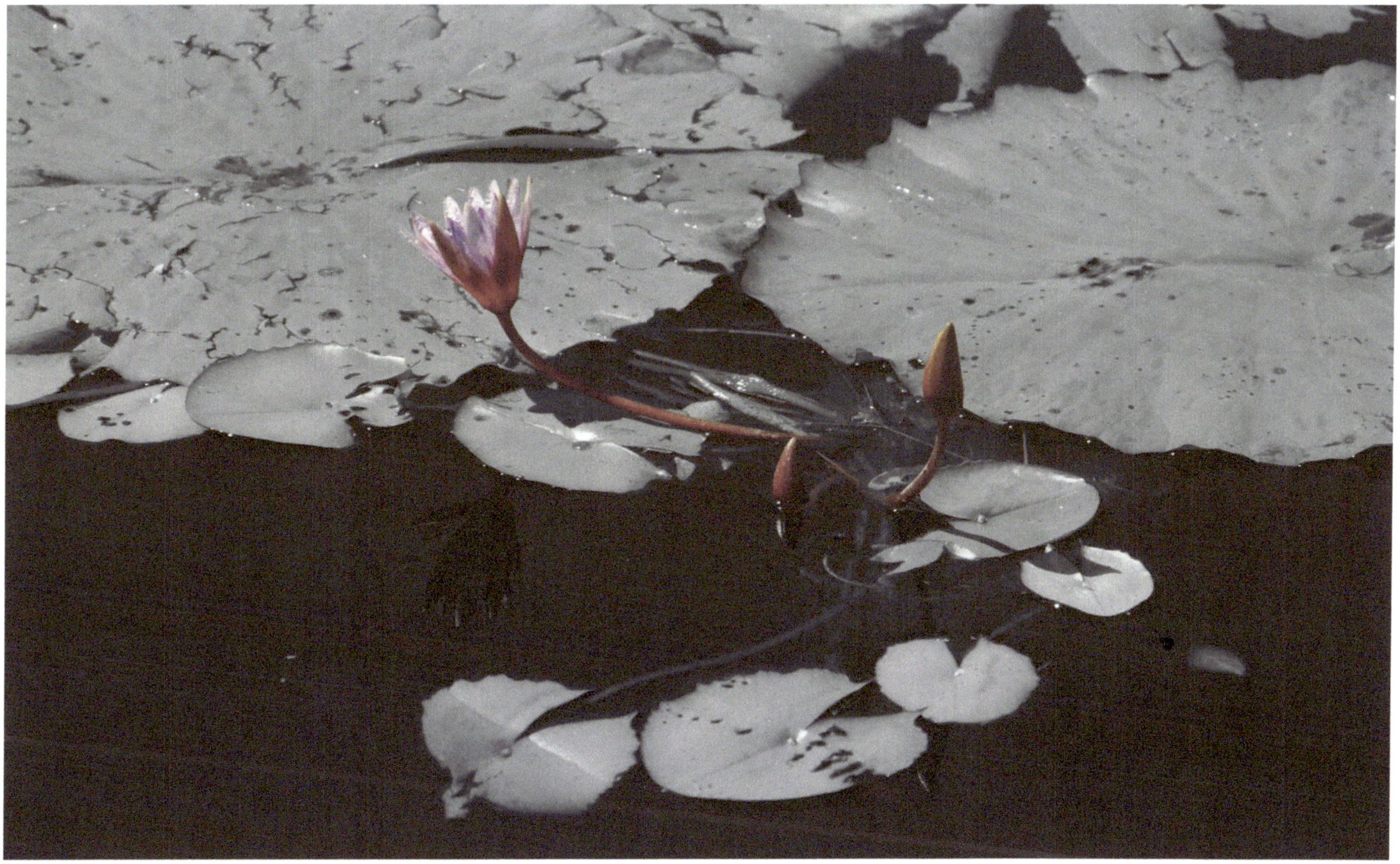

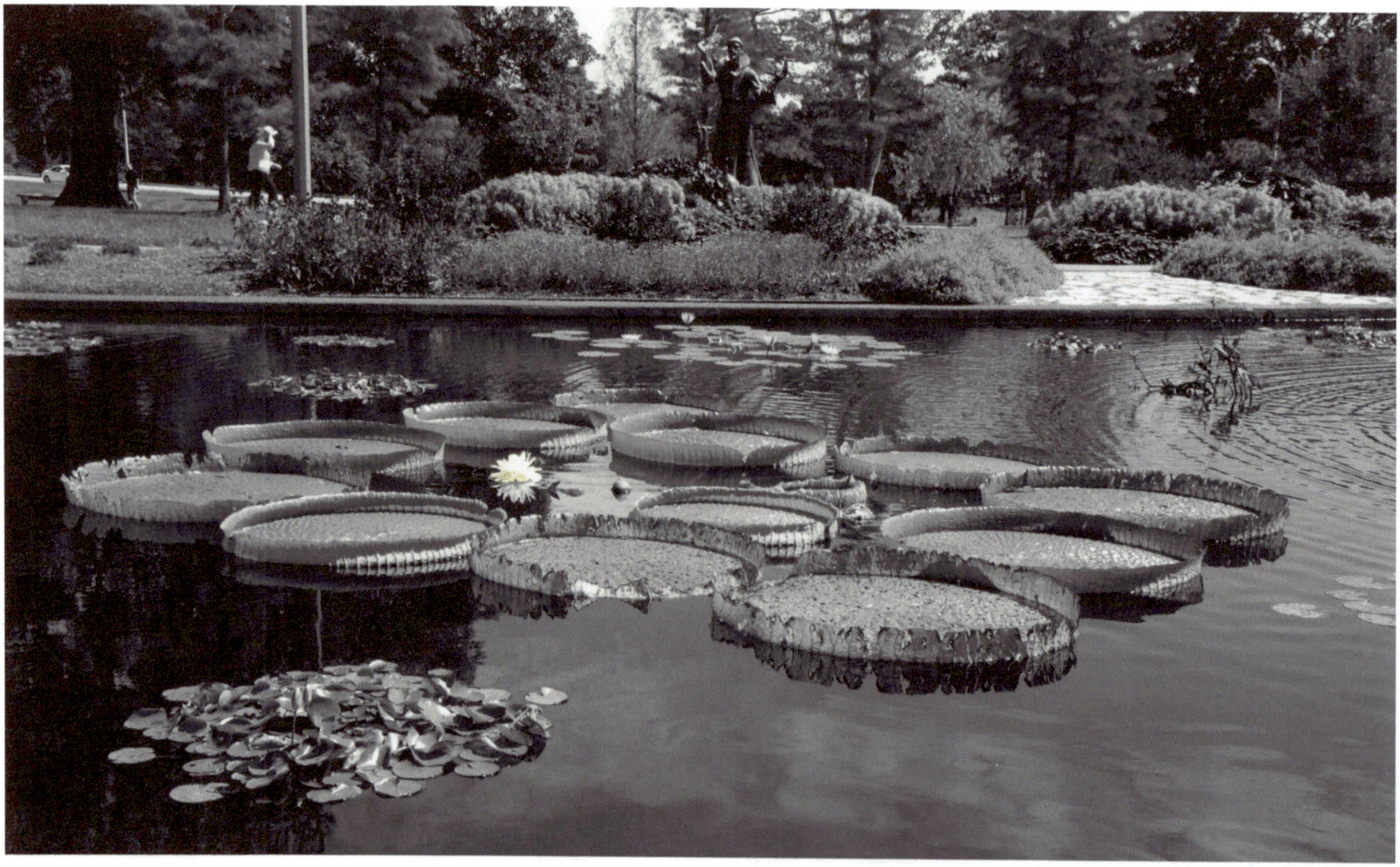

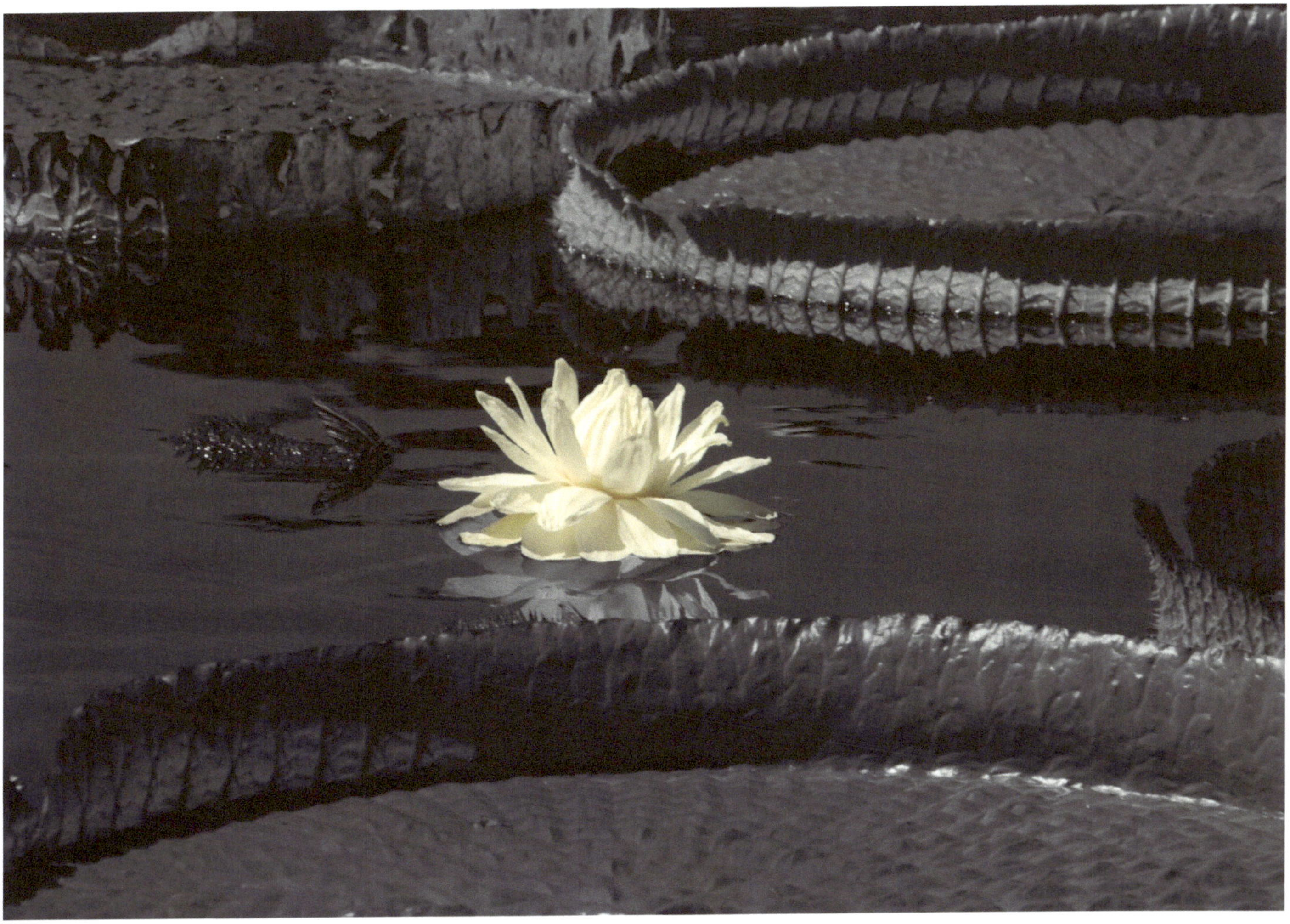

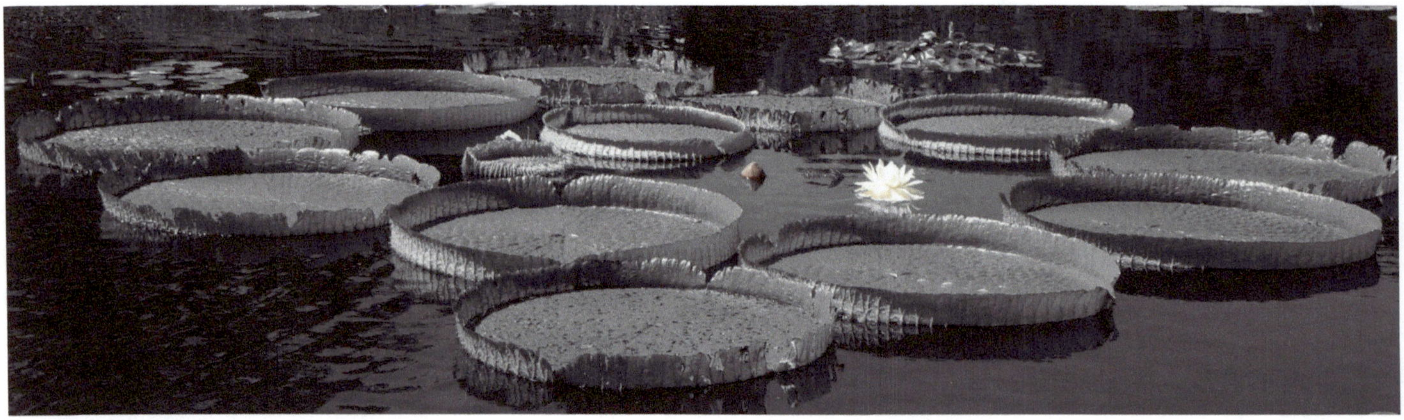

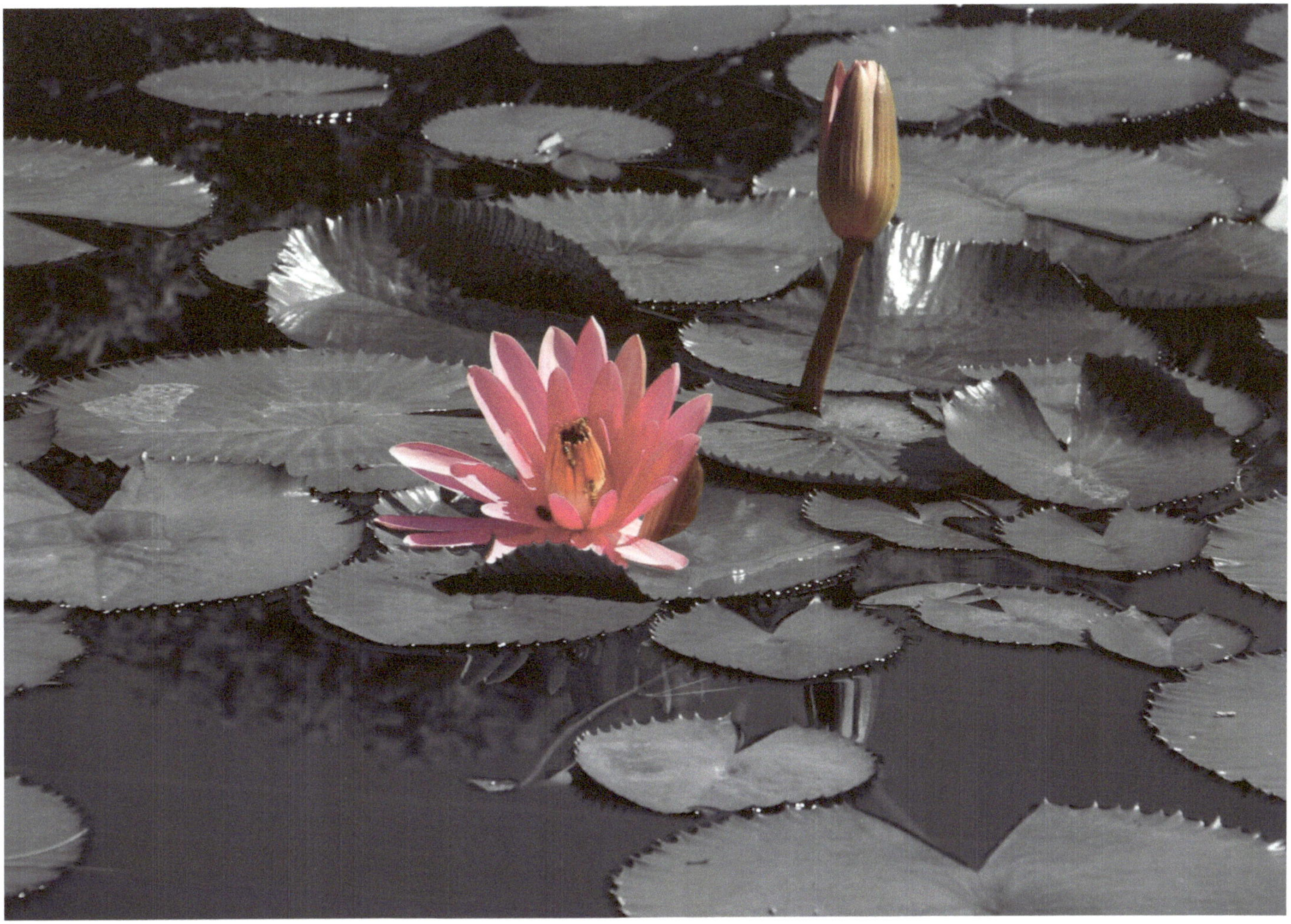

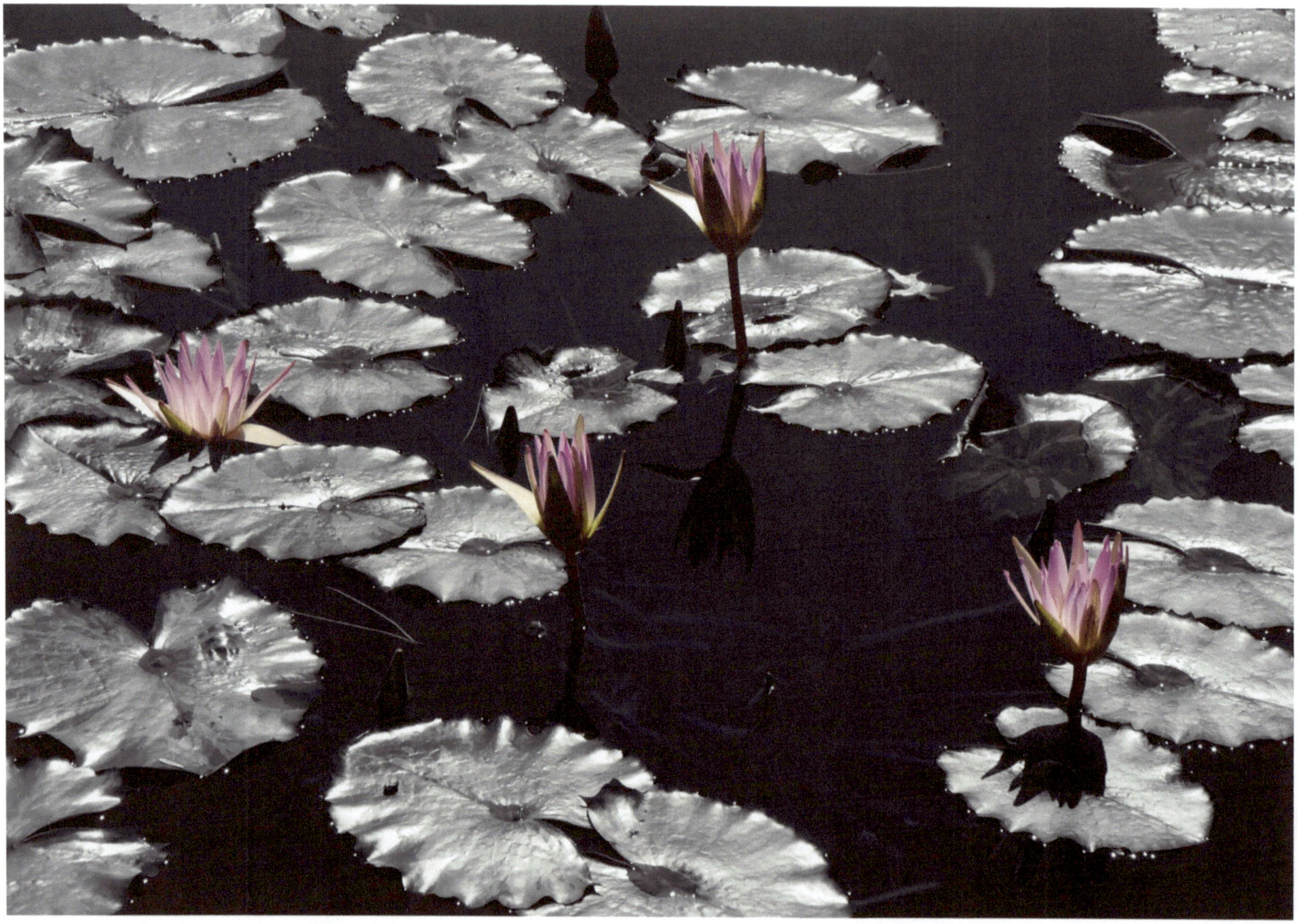

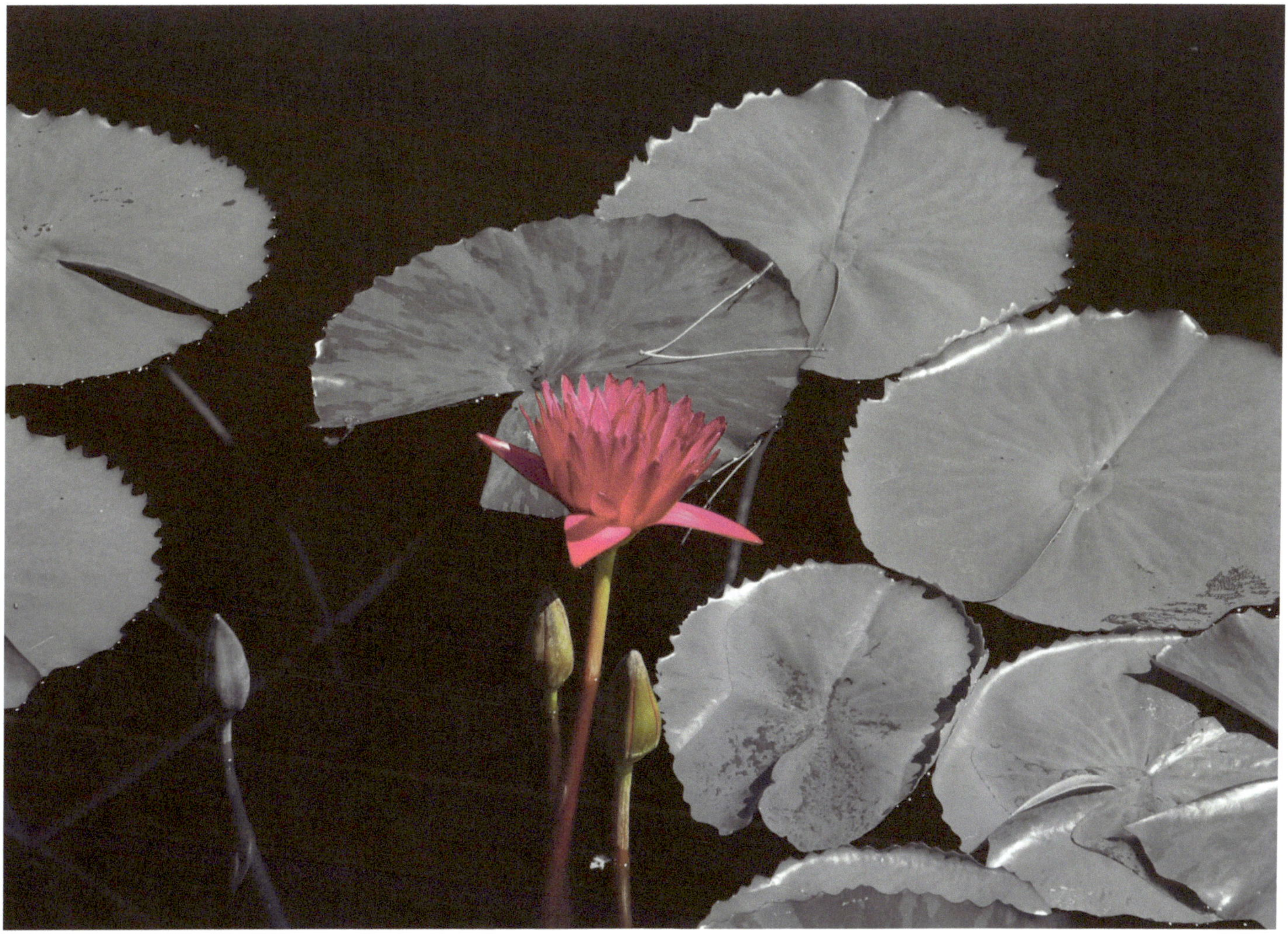

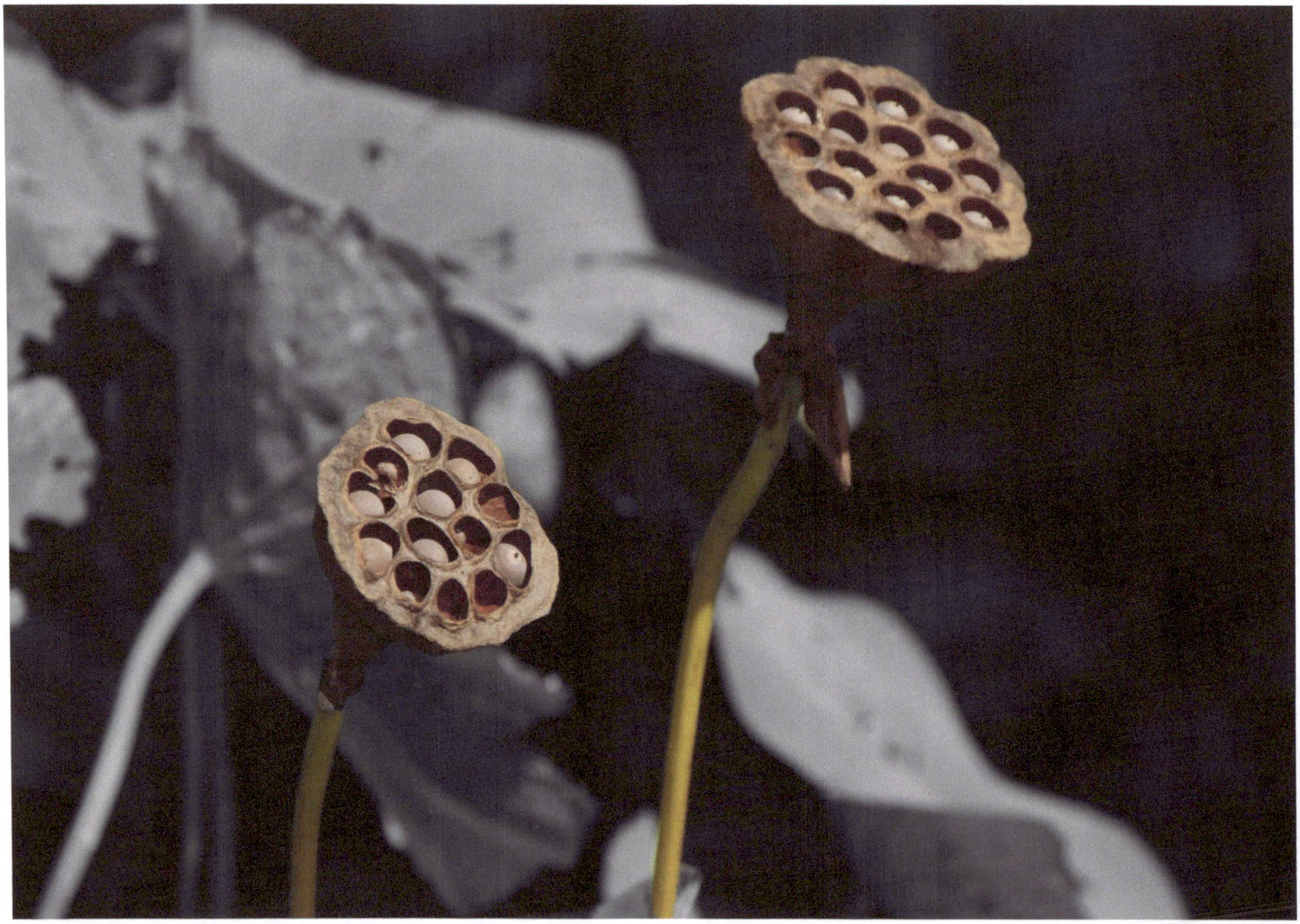

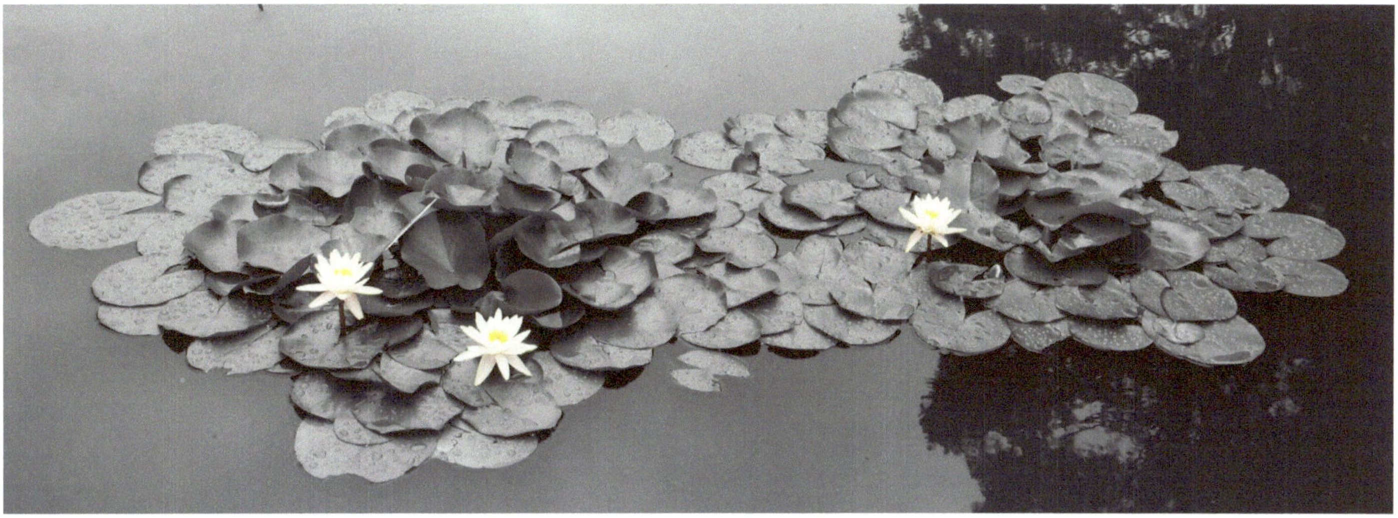

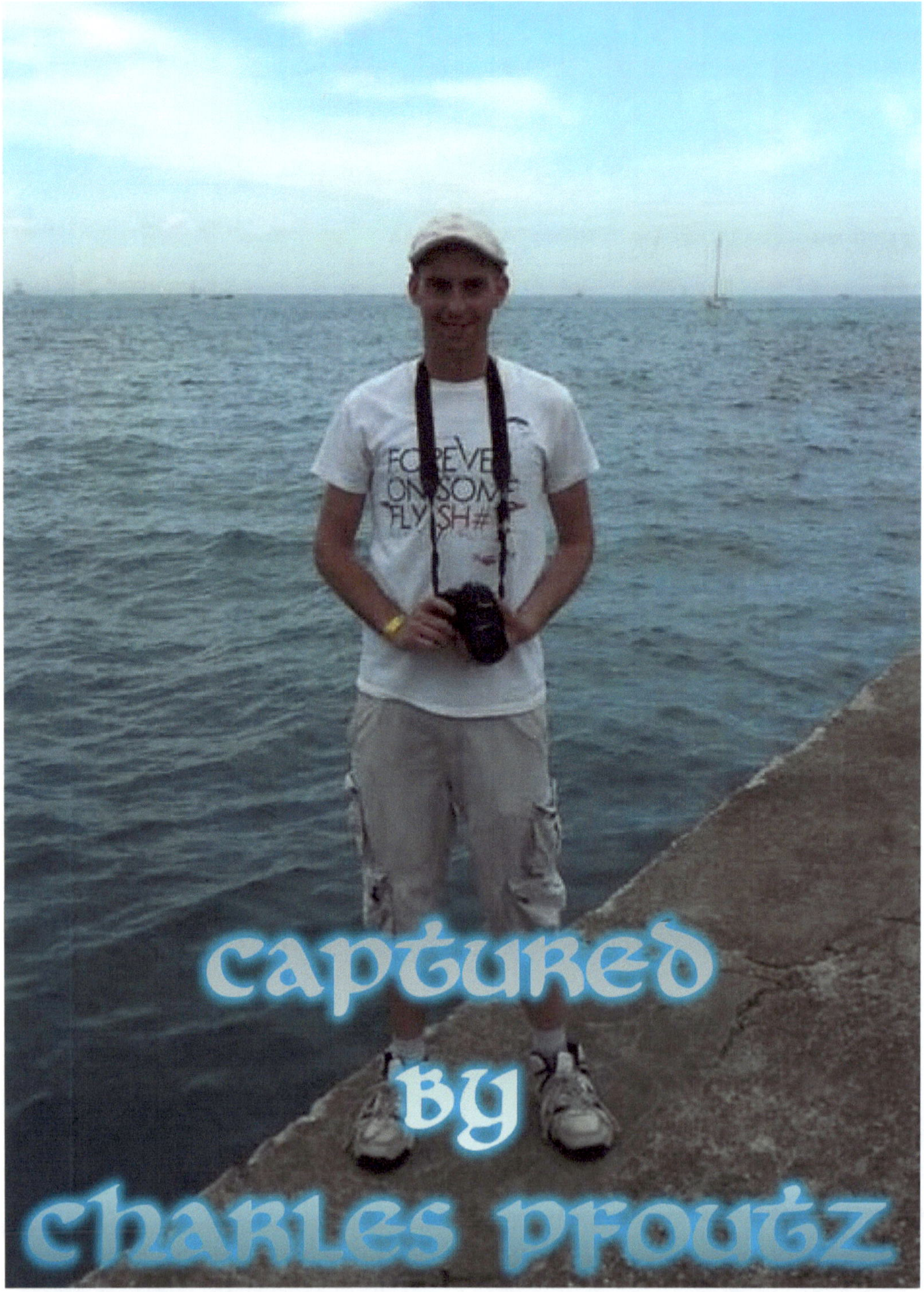
Captured
By
Charles Pfoutz

www.ingramcontent.com/pod-product-compliance
Lightning Source LLC
Chambersburg PA
CBHW040742200526
45159CB00023B/1581
9781519133557